COURT DISHES

OF

CHINA

清宮藥譜

景嘉 題

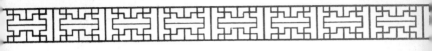

COURT DISHES
OF
CHINA

The Cuisine of the Ch'ing Dynasty

SU CHUNG
(LUCILLE DAVIS)

Photographs by

MIKI TAKAGI • KENNETH F. DAVIS

CHARLES E. TUTTLE COMPANY: PUBLISHERS
Rutland, Vermont   Tokyo, Japan

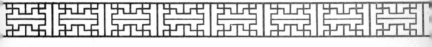

Representatives
Continental Europe: BOXERBOOKS, INC., Zurich
British Isles: PRENTICE-HALL INTERNATIONAL, INC., London
Australasia: PAUL FLESCH & CO., PTY. LTD., Melbourne

Published by the Charles E. Tuttle Company, Inc.
of Rutland, Vermont & Tokyo, Japan
with editorial offices at
Suido 1-chome, 2-6, Bunkyo-ku, Tokyo, Japan

PRINTED IN JAPAN

TO THOSE WHO ARE FOND OF
GOOD FOOD

CONTENTS

PLATES

FOREWORD

My Chinese dinners have always been popular with our friends, and, whenever our guests learned that the dishes were prepared from old recipes from ancient dynasties, they always asked how I acquired these rare recipes. Since the question might also be asked by the readers of this book, I will begin by giving a little of my background and the source of the recipes.

Just two weeks before the closing of the American consulate in Peking in April, 1950, the American consul general anxiously ordered the evacuation of the handful of Americans there because the anti-American feeling of Communist China had increased. I was then married to the second grandson of the great scholar and poet Cheng Hsiao-hsü who had been in turn a tutor, a minister of the imperial household, prime minister, as well as a relative by marriage to the former emperor of China, Hsüan T'ung (last of the Ch'ing dynasty and later Henry Pu-yi, ruler of Manchukuo). Because of grandfather Cheng's exemplary services and great loyalty, regardless of the former emperor's status, his imperial highness insisted that their two families be united through the marriage of his younger sister Princess Jun Ho and Cheng Kuan Yüan, eldest grandson of the scholar. My marriage to his second grandson was welcomed by grandfather Cheng because my husband had acquired a great fondness for Americans during his college days at St. John's University in Shanghai where he was taught by American professors. Grandfather was pleased that his grandson had married a girl who was not only born and brought up in the West, but who also had some knowledge of the Orient, my husband and I having met at a Waseda University reception in Tokyo, Japan.

In 1950, unfortunately, circumstances in China changed to such an extent that my American citizenship and Japanese parentage were placing in jeopardy not only myself but also the family into which I had married. After much consideration and with the greatest reluctance and sorrow, I decided there was no other course open for me but to leave China. When I said goodbye to my sister-in-law, the former Princess Jun Ho, she told me, "When you reach Japan, you must call on the Japanese imperial family and extend to them our sincerest regards. You must also get in touch with Princess Aichingioro and give her whatever help you can." Princess Aichingioro, daughter of the former Marquis Saga of Japan, had in 1936 married former Prince P'u Chieh, younger brother of Hsüan T'ung. At the end of World War II, when her husband and his brother were made political prisoners, the princess had returned to Japan with her two daughters. In 1950 both men were still imprisoned. Soon after my arrival in Japan, I called on Madame Toryu Takao whose husband had been the Japanese ambassador to China for many years and who is a close friend of the imperial families of both Japan and China. Accompanied by Madame Takao, I conveyed my sister-in-law's greetings to the various members of the Japanese imperial family, and it was through Madame Takao that I was able to locate Princess Aichingioro, to whom, during these past years, I have become very devoted.

In 1957, after the tragic death of her beautiful elder daughter, it became urgent to divert the princess's mind from her overwhelming grief. After much discussion and through the persuasion of her parents and myself, she agreed to write a book of her experiences in Manchukuo and her desperate flight after its fall. This book, published in Japanese in 1960, proved a bestseller, running into eight editions. After that she began to compile a cookbook, based on recipes she had collected and on an old cookbook she had been given by a faithful Manchurian retainer. Before she could complete her work, she learned early in 1961 that her husband had been released from prison but would not be permitted to leave China. The only way she could be with him was to go to Peking, where, after sixteen years of separation, she and her daughter were at last reunited with the former Prince P'u Chieh. Just before her departure, she turned over to me her collection of menus, recipes, and other data, and said, "I hope that you will complete this material for I'm sure the world would like to know the real story behind Peking cooking as it was developed by the imperial families of China."

For a while I was dubious of my ability to compile a book on Chinese cookery for the only experience I had was acquired long ago when I was severely reprimanded by my mother-in-law for being found in the kitchen watching the expert cooks prepare delicious Chinese food. It was considered extremely unlady-like in China for a member of the family to be in the kitchen. However, my American upbringing would not permit me to let such a wonderful culinary opportunity escape. Thereafter, in spite of my well-meaning mother-in-law, I cautiously observed our cooks and took many notes, never realizing at the time that my inquisitive mind would help me later to reproduce the old recipes of the imperial families in this book. I have thoroughly enjoyed kitchen-testing, converting the measurements to Western standards, and adapting these recipes to an easy-to-follow style for your pleasure.

The preparation of this book has been made possible through the assistance of many friends. Vice Admiral William Marshall, U.S.N., retired, president of the Bourbon Institute and a collector of rare recipes, on one of his visits to our house encouraged and advised me to compile the unusual recipes as soon as possible. Professor Ching Chia, a cousin of the former emperor, wrote the beautiful calligraphy for the title page the meaning of which is ''Court Dishes of the Ch'ing Dynasty.'' Mrs. Lynn Katoh, the well-known writer, has graciously looked over my manuscript and given me helpful advice. General Shang Chen, of the Chinese Nationalist government, retired, and Admiral Wang Shih Leh, formerly of the Imperial Chinese Navy, sampled many of the dishes for their authenticity. Through the introduction by Mrs. Mitsuo Sato, wife of the abbot of the Kotoku Temple in Kamakura (site of the famous Great Buddha), I have been privileged to photograph and use as illustrations rare old Chinese ceramics in Mr. Matsushige Hirota's collection in Kita-Kamakura. Through the courtesy of Mr. Seizo Hayashiya, noted authority on Chinese ceramics at the Tokyo National Museum in Ueno Park, Tokyo, I was permitted to photograph parts of their collection. Lastly, my husband's encouragement and interest have added tremendously in making the realization of this book possible.

THE

IMPERIAL CUISINE

The summit of the Chinese cuisine of the Ch'ing Dynasty (1644–1912) was reached during the reign of Emperor Ch'ien-lung who ruled from 1736 to 1796. The tables of other emperors never equalled that of Ch'ien-lung in magnificence. The Ch'ing, originally Manchurian, did not, in their early stage, attach much importance to culinary arts. However, these flourished during the reign of Ch'ien-lung, and, for this reason, interesting recipes of that period are included in this book.

No one in any dynasty of China ever lived a more rigidly controlled life than the emperor of the Ch'ing. Due to strict observance of traditional conventions of the court, the freedom of the emperor was far less than that of an ordinary man. When he lived in the Imperial Palace, he had to rise at four o'clock. This early rising was called *ch'ing chia,* meaning "Your appearance is begged in court." At four o'clock, a eunuch, whose sole duty was to announce, "It's time for *ch'ing chia,*" made his announcement. Waited upon by another eunuch, the emperor bathed, ate a dish of crystal sugar and edible swallows' nests, cooked together over high heat. He then proceeded to attend the early audience which he gave to courtiers daily in the Tai Ho Tien Hall. From his chambers to the hall he rode on a palanquin, four guards in front and several eunuchs in the rear, and returned in the same manner. He then slept again until seven o'clock and at nine he had breakfast. An old record lists the following menu for May 10, 1754, the 18th year of Ch'ien-lung's reign:

Main Course Dishes

A dish of a fat chicken, pot-boiled duck, and bean curd, cooked by Chang Erh

A dish of swallows' nests and julienned smoked duck, cooked by Chang Erh

A bowl of clear soup, cooked by Jung Kuei

A dish of julienned pot-boiled chicken, cooked by Jung Kuei

A dish of smoked fat chicken and Chinese cabbage, cooked by Chang Erh

A dish of salted duck and pork, cooked by Jung Kuei

A dish of court-style fried chicken

Pastries

A dish of bamboo-stuffed steamed dumplings

A dish of rice cakes

A dish of rice cakes with honey

Pickles

*Served in a ceramic container patterned
with hollyhock flowers*

Chinese cabbage pickled in brine

Cucumbers preserved in soy

Pickled eggplant

Rice

Boiled rice

Emperor Ch'ien-lung's reign was the golden age of the Ch'ing Dynasty. However, judging from the above menu, one cannot say that the meal was luxurious, and it was not as extravagant as imperial meals are often described. For example, Madame Te Ling, author of a well-known book on the imperial court, reported that Empress Dowager Tzu-hsi's meal consisted of over one hundred dishes.

After breakfast, the emperor carefully studied documents submitted by his ministers and promulgated instructions which were sent to Chün-chi-ch'u (Military Plans Office). Then he granted an imperial interview to officials and consulted Manchurian and Chinese ministers of Chün-chi-ch'u about important state affairs. Unlike the morning audience, which was a kind of a ceremony, during Chün-chi problems of politics were debated. It was sometimes one o'clock when Chün-chi was over, and the emperor returned to his chambers or to some other house to have refreshments. Lunch was served between two and three in the afternoon. The amount and the kinds of dishes were almost the same as the breakfast. After lunch, the emperor usually took a nap for about an hour, another traditional custom. In the afternoon, he frequently held *yeh chien,* that is, discussions and lectures with well-known scholars, or he conversed with the empress dowager, the empress, or some of his consorts. The only amusements the emperor could enjoy in the court were to attend a stage show, to practice calligraphy, and to paint. No other amusements were permitted.

What was most unpleasant for the emperor was that, although he could dine with the empress dowager, the empress and his consorts were not permitted to sit at the table with him. The emperor was permitted to go to the empress's palace or to his consorts', but such visits entailed a great deal of trouble. His visit had to be announced in advance by a eunuch, and, when he arrived, the empress or consort had to be waiting on her knees in front of her palace. Entering the palace, the emperor went up to the throne (which was not installed in ordinary palace buildings) and received his consort's salute of "three-kneeling-and-nine-bows." It was because of such trouble that the emperor rarely visited his empress's or consorts' buildings when he was within the court, and, most of the time, the lady was invited to the emperor's chambers. When the emperor wished to see one of his consorts, he invited her to supper. A record, written in the 38th year of Emperor Ch'ien-lung's era, mentions that "there was an Imperial Order to grant a supper to Imperial Consort Shun," and is evidence that the emperor received the imperial consort in his chambers on that night.

As long as the emperor stayed within the court, he was restricted in every way by tradition. Consequently, it was only natural that the emperors wished to stay away from court as much as possible. When the emperor lived in a detached palace, he could lead a comparatively free life, for he was exempted from the early morning audience, he could dine with his consorts, and every manner and custom was simplified. Nevertheless, he was not as free as an ordinary person, for he still had to give daily audiences and promulgate instructions concerning the documents submitted to him. However, he could not live away from the court long, for if he enjoyed himself a little too much, a letter of expostulation was sure to come from the prime minister.

Meals for the emperor were not as fabulous as is generally imagined by outsiders, but the system of preparing them was on an extraordinarily large scale. The emperor's dietary life came under the jurisdiction of the Office of the Imperial Household to which the imperial cuisine belonged. The imperial cuisine consisted of five divisions: fish and meat, vegetables, roasts, refreshments, and rice. The divisions were divided into two sections, each having a chef and five cooks. In addition, each division included a supervisor, charged with watching over the cooks, and an accountant whose responsibility was the procurement of materials and the accounting for them.

The imperial cuisine of the Ch'ing Dynasty developed its cooking methods and style mainly from three different parts of China:

1. *Shantung*. The fact that the Ming dynasty (1368–1644) had employed Shantung cooks for over two hundred years while they held court at Peking had popularized Shantung dishes in the court as well as with the

general public. Many of these Ming court dishes were retained after the Ch'ing took over the sovereignty. There was nothing specifically Pekinese in this cookery.

2. *Manchuria*. The Manchurians, originally nomads, used mutton and various game fowl and animals in preparing their meals. After the Ch'ing, formerly Manchus, became rulers of China, the cooks of the imperial cuisine improved upon the Manchurian dishes by producing unique flavors. Although mutton dishes date back to those days, they are now known and famous as Peking dishes.

3. *South China*. Emperor Ch'ien-lung made two tours of southern China, both times to Soochow and Hangchow. Because these two provinces were so prosperous there was a proverb that, while above is heaven, Soochow is heaven on earth. These people gave the emperor a most enthusiastic welcome, and he took such a special liking for Soochow dishes that he ordered a menu of them to be made. Later, he sent for a cook from Soochow and made him an imperial cook for his tour of northeast China during the forty-third year of his reign.

The greatest difficulty in serving the emperor came from the fact that there was no regular place for him to eat. The imperial cuisine was required to serve meals whenever and wherever the emperor demanded. For example, when the emperor was taking a walk, men of the refreshment division had to follow him with two round bamboo baskets containing plenty of refreshments, tea, and a small stove so that food might be ready within minutes after it was ordered. To meet such requirements, the imperial cuisine provided two devices not to be found elsewhere. One was a portable cooking range and the other was a heating pot of which there were two types. The first, for winter use, consisted of two beautifully made silver bowls, one of which was laid on top of the other, the upper bowl for food and the lower one for hot water. The other was an iron bowl about a half-inch thick with two very thick iron plates. Cooked food was placed in the iron bowl, then one highly heated iron plate was placed under the bowl and the other on top of the bowl. When the emperor was served, food was immediately transferred from the iron bowl into a porcelain bowl.

Much attention was paid to the temperature of the emperor's meal. Rice, rice-gruel or refreshments were, as a matter of course, cooked by the rice or refreshments division, but they were served by eunuchs. When serving, a eunuch placed the food in bowls on a side table at which time he tested the temperature of the food by placing his hand on the outer side of the bowls before placing them on the emperor's table.

The cooks took particular care of the emperor's likes and dislikes which differed from emperor to emperor. When the emperor enjoyed a particular food, it was prepared every day. Emperor Ch'ien-lung enjoyed Soochow and duck dishes, so they were always found in the daily menus. On the contrary, because he disliked shark's fin dishes, one does not find them in the court menus during his reign.

The name of the cook was always written on the menu so that the same food might be requested at any time. This system was also convenient when the emperor wished to reward a cook for certain foods he particularly appreciated. This custom was observed from the earliest Manchurian days in China up to the end of Manchukuo. Every day the steward of the imperial cuisine took notes of the likes and dislikes of the emperor as well as the exact amount he ate, reported this information to the minister of imperial household, and then kept the record in the warehouse. There were four warehouses-of-the-steward in the court where such records were kept together with records relating to clothing and housing as well as to his activities. The records concerning food were the most extensive.

Bestowal of dishes, especially on the emperor's favorite consort, was a custom within the court, but it was unusual for the emperor to give dishes of food to those outside the court. This, however, was the opportunity for the cooks to earn money. It is said that when Empress Dowager Tzu-hsi bestowed a duck dish on Yüan Shikai, a powerful member of the Imperial Court, he gave 10,000 silver liangs (one liang purchased 50 eggs) to the cook who delivered the dish.

The cooks of the imperial cuisine were for the most part Manchurians whose positions were hereditary during the three hundred years of the Ch'ing Dynasty, but there were also some who came from Chechiang Province during the period of Emperor Ch'ien-lung. The cooks' homes were mostly located at Hai Tien, west of Peking, where, with their families, they formed a very sound and special community. After the abdication of the last emperor of the Ch'ing Dynasty, many of those houses fell, but some of the enterprising cooks opened restaurants. Others followed the ex-Emperor Hsüan T'ung and later became cooks of the imperial cuisine of the court of Manchukuo.

Remuneration for the cooks of the imperial cuisine was not as high as was generally conjectured. The monthly pay of the average cook was only five or six silver liangs. However, they made up for their limited incomes by selling leftovers, as the office of the imperial household relegated such matters to the cooks. When the empress dowager, inquisitive by nature and entirely against the code of conduct of an empress dowager, had the account of the imperial cuisine audited, she found that an egg on her table cost her two silver liangs. In those days, as noted above, one liang would buy 50 eggs in the public market.

Unlike other Manchus, those belonging to the office of the imperial household were domestic servants of the emperor and were subject to many restrictions. As a result, those servants were always seeking means to gain from the emperor's purse. The emperor, subject to the imperial code of conduct, could not interfere in pecuniary matters, and, since the governmental offices outside of the court had no right to inquire about finances, etc., the servants of the imperial household flourished. After the emperor lost his political power, though the court survived for some years, Manchurian officials in general lost their means of livelihood, but the Manchus of the office of imperial household were still wealthy and continued to take charge of court business. According to Prince P'u Chieh, Emperor Hsüan T'ung and he often planned to go abroad to observe social conditions, but each time their intention was frustrated by the opposition from those Manchus of the office of the imperial household who would have lost their secret sources of income if the emperor left the Forbidden City of Peking.

In 1936 when Princess Aichingioro left Japan for Manchukuo, the empress dowager, mother of the present emperor of Japan, asked that she learn to prepare Chinese court dishes and inform the Japanese imperial cuisine of the recipes. The princess' husband, Prince P'u Chieh, made arrangements for Cheng Yung, Supreme Chef of the Court, to give her the recipes of the imperial court of China and instruct her in their preparation. These recipes, along with others she collected, are published in English for the first time in this book.

NOTE: Chinese names are based on the Wade system, and in accordance with oriental custom surnames precede given names.

A
FORMAL BANQUET

In China it was customary when giving a formal dinner or banquet to send an invitation, inscribed in gold on heavy red paper, folded in four, and listing the names of the people invited, by messenger to each of the guests. Whether it was accepted or not, the invitation had to be acknowledged. This was a practical arrangement, for if one found that he did not like any of the listed guests, he could decline the invitation, thus eliminating a boring or tiresome occasion.

Seating arrangements were important at a formal dinner. The place nearest the family altar or the place furthest from the door was considered the seat of honor. The host sat opposite the guest of honor in the lowest position, and the left-hand side of the host was considered higher than the right-hand side.

The hostess would direct the cook to select the very best from the land, sea, and air to please her guests. In doing so, she included a bit of everything: meat, vegetables, flowers, fruits, fowl, game, fish, shellfish, sea weed, and even birds' nests. The number of courses ranged from 7 to 49. A formal dinner used to start with 8 to 16 cold dishes, called *ya tsuo ts'ai* (sitting duck food), but nowadays, one platter containing 4 to 6 kinds of cold foods is usually served. The name of the dinner would depend upon the name of the main dish: it might be called shark's fin dinner, swallows' nests dinner or sea cucumber dinner.

During the first 3 main courses the host, after each

dish, would circulate from table to table inviting everyone to take wine with him. From then on the guests helped themselves. The guests played games, particularly drinking games, after the 5 main dishes were served. The last main dish was usually a whole fish. This custom came about because the phonetic meaning of the word fish is ''more'', indicating ''while this is all for now, we will invite you again another time.'' At the end of the dinner, the guests thanked the host and the hostess for their graciousness and the wonderful dinner.

On the pages that follow I have set forth some suggested menus for various types of Chinese dinners and lunches.

MENUS

Crab Meat Egg Roll
Arc Shellfish and Celery
Bamboo Shoots and Mushrooms Fried and Simmered with Soy
Fried and Steamed Pork with Skin
Chicken and Cucumber with Sauce
Fried Shrimps
Excellent Casserole
Fried Smoked Fish
Abalone and Asparagus
Chestnuts and Chinese Cabbage
Steamed Buns with Filling
Almond Curd with Fruit Cocktail

Deep-Fried Fish
Walnuts and Chicken Cubes
Sweet, Sour, and Hot Chinese Cabbage
Boiled Mutton
Day Lilies Cooked with Julienned Pork
Chicken, Bamboo, and Mushroom Soup
Lotus Leaf Porridge

Steamed Flounder
Fried Chicken Cubes
Fried Turnip
Braised Head of Tiger
Fried Bamboo Shoot, Mushroom, and Cucumber

Pickled Vegetable Root Soup
Family Pancake or Rice
Red Bean Porridge

Pork Liver Cooked with Five Spices
Fried Skin of Bean Curd Cooked with Starch Dressing
Steamed Carp
Fried Chicken with Peppercorns
Stuffed Marrow
Rolls or Rice

Stewed Crab Meat
Steamed Duck with Mushroom
Deep Fried Meat Balls
Steamed Brocade-like Array of Vegetables with Bean Curd
Ham and Marrow Soup
Fried and Cooked Eggplant
Buns or Rice

Fried Prawns
Chicken Cooked with Bean Curd
Stewed String Beans
Swallows' Nests Soup
Crucian Carp Seasoned with Red Pepper Sauce
Spring Pancake or Rice

SNACK OR LUNCH MENUS

Fried Noodles with Prawns
Fried Chicken Fillet with Eggwhite
Chinese Cabbage Soup

Steamed Dumplings with Crabmeat Filling
Sweet and Sour Cucumbers
River Ball Soup

*Miniature Dumplings with Chicken and Mushroom
    Filling*
Chicken and Shrimps
*Fried and Cooked Carrots, Pork, Soy Beans, and Bean
    Curd*
Soy Bean and Bean Curd

NOTE: Many of the recipes require increasing when prepared for large groups, while others require decreasing for fewer guests. It is difficult to determine just how many people may be served with the menus I have suggested, for much depends upon the guests' appetite and their calorie consciousness. Most people who eat Chinese food disregard the quantity and enjoy this adventure in eating. Recently, I invited 14 people to dinner and prepared what I assumed was enough for 24 guests, but the food was just enought for the 14! They enjoyed the dinner so much that they were oblivious of the amount they ate. Therefore, I hesitate to state how many people may be served with each menu but will trust your good judgment.

FOOD SELECTION
AND
PREPARATION

Listed below are some general instructions on the selection and preparation of foods for court dishes of the Ch'ing dynasty.

1. For mutton dishes, use shanks for braising, loin for frying and chopping, shoulder for stewing, and leg for roasting. Beef is not included in this book as it was considered a sacrilege in the olden days to eat beef. To kill cattle was comparable to killing a man who tills the soil to produce food, for much of the land was cultivated with the help of cattle. However, since times have changed, beef may be substituted if desired for recipes requiring mutton.

2. For pork dishes, use loin, shoulder, and ham portions for braising and roasting, shoulder for stewing, bacon and loin chops for chopping, and the butt and spareribs for stock.

3. For chicken dishes, use poulards or capons for braising and roasting, fryers for frying, stewing chickens for stewing and for stock.

4. To determine freshness when purchasing fish, examine the eyes to see if they are clear. Stale fish have cloudy eyes and are dark under the gills.

5. Always wash fish with salt and water to remove surface film.

6. In court cuisine, meats, fish, and vegetables are cut in sizes that can be easily manipulated with chopsticks. They are chopped, cubed, julienned, or sliced.

7. Arrange all ingredients on a tray in the sequence of their use to simplify cooking procedure.

8. When frying, pre-heat iron pan first and then add oil. Heat to boiling point or until smoking ceases. This eliminates a raw oily flavor and prevents food from adhering to the pan.

9. There are exceptions, but, when frying, onion and ginger are browned before other ingredients are added.

10. Fresh green vegetables are fried rapidly, stirring briskly over high heat to retain their freshness and crispness.

11. Except for julienned meats, meats are cooked until they all but fall apart.

12. There are exceptions but, on the whole, the cooks of the imperial kitchen strove to bring out the flavor of the main ingredient by using chicken stock for a chicken dish, fish stock for a fish dish, pork stock for a pork dish, and vegetable stock for a vegetable dish.

13. Japanese Kikkoman soy has been used in all recipes requiring soy in this book. Since non-oriental soy is highly concentrated, it must be diluted before using.

14. If the quantity of soy, as directed in the recipes, is found insufficient, add salt instead of more soy to prevent darkening the color of the food.

15. One teaspoon of salt is used to cook 1 pound of meat. However, 6 pounds of meat do not require 2 tablespoons of salt. Therefore, season to taste.

16. Monosodium glutamate, commercially known as Ajinomoto, was used in many of the recipes, but Ac'cent or Vetsin may be substituted.

17. The number of persons the various dishes will serve has been determined by the Western "rule of thumb" of a half pound of meat, fish, or fowl per person. However, in old China, many dishes were served at each meal, and the guests partook of small portions of each

dish. For example, when there were six for dinner, six different dishes would be served, along with one or two bowls of soup and rice, noodles, or steamed bread.

The measurements used in these recipes are as follows:

$$3 \text{ teaspoons} = 1 \text{ tablespoon}$$
$$4 \text{ tablespoons} = \tfrac{1}{4} \text{ cup}$$
$$16 \text{ tablespoons} = 1 \text{ cup}$$
$$2 \text{ cups} = 1 \text{ pint}$$
$$2 \text{ pints} = 1 \text{ quart}$$
$$4 \text{ quarts} = 1 \text{ gallon}$$

SPECIAL
INGREDIENTS
AND
METHODS

In the recipes that follow there are some foods which may not be familiar to the cook who is venturing into a new culinary sphere and others that require special methods of preparation. Substitutes are suggested for those items that may not be available at local markets. A list of shops specializing in Oriental foods will be found at the end of this book. If ordering by mail, it is a good idea to use both Chinese and English names.

agar-agar *(yang fen)* sold in powder form and in thin white strips. Substitute gelatine.

almond powder *(hsing jen fen)*, canned.

arc shellfish *(ch'ing chih ke)*, fresh. Shell, remove black edges, wash with salt water. Substitute clams or other shellfish.

bamboo shoots *(chu sun)*, canned. Cut in half and remove the calcium deposit in the center. Use only the tender portion.

bamboo shoots, dried and preserved with salt *(yü lan p'ien)*. Steep in hot water for 40 minutes, rinse many times in cold water to eliminate salt, and drain.

bean curd *(tou fu)*, fresh or canned.

bean curd, dried *(tung tou fu)*. Steep in hot water for 10 minutes and press firmly to remove water.

bean curd, fermented with salt, spices, and red malt *(chiang tou fu)*, canned.

bean curd, fermented, white *(fu ju)*, canned.

bean curd skin, dried *(tou fu p'i)*. Steep in hot water until tender and drain.

bean curd skin, fresh *(tou szu)*, julienned.

bean sprouts *(tou ya)*, fresh or canned.

beans, red *(hung tou)*, dried.

beans, salted *(tou ch'ih)*, salted. Steep in hot water a few minutes, then drain.

beefsteak plant *(tzu jin ts'ai)*, fresh. Substitute lettuce or other greens.

birds' nests, see swallows' nests.

carp, crucian *(li yü)*. Substitute any fresh water fish.

chicken, smoked *(hsün chi)*. Use either of the following methods: (1) After lighting 1 tablespoon brandy and 1 cup sugar per pound of chicken in an earthen pot 12" deep and 14" or more in diameter, place the chicken on a dish or rack raised an inch or two from the burning sugar. Cover tightly, seal, and smoke for 25 to 30 minutes per pound; or (2) Smoke a 2-pound chicken on a rack in an earthen pot with live charcoal and pine needles or hickory wheels (soaked in water for a few hours) in an earthen barbecue pit covered with a heavy earthen cover for 50 to 60 minutes. A 4 pound chicken is smoked for 2 hours, etc.

Chinese cabbage, fresh *(pai ts'ai)*. Remove tough outer leaves before using.

Chinese doughnuts *(yu t'iao)*. Mix well into a dough 1 cup sifted flour, 2 teaspoons baking powder, 1/8 teaspoon alum, 1/8 teaspoon salt, and ½ cup water. Form into doughnuts 1" thick and 2" in diameter. Fry until crisp.

Chinese ham *(huo t'ui)*, cured or canned. Substitute Smithfield ham.

Chinese vermicelli *(fen szu)*. Made of green bean powder.

chrysanthemum flowers *(chiu hua)*, fresh or dried. When using dried, steep in hot water 10 minutes and drain.

cuttlefish, fresh *(yü yü)*. Remove tentacles, head, bones, and caudal fins. Wash body of fish and place in bowl with 3 cups hot water and 1 teaspoon soda. Cover tightly and place in a warm spot for 2 days. Remove from bowl, rinse, drain.

dates, Chinese, dried *(tsao)*.

day lilies, dried *(huang hua)*. These are wild flowers and are small in size. Soak in water for 20 minutes, wash, drain, and remove bottom half-inch of stems.

dove eggs, fresh *(ke tzu tan)*. Substitute quail or chicken eggs in smaller quantity. Chicken eggs should be quartered before serving.

fish, smoked *(hsün yü)*. As with smoked chicken, there are two methods: (1) After lighting 1 tablespoon brandy and 1 cup sugar per pound of fish in an earthen pot 12" deep and 14" or more in diameter, place the fish on a dish or rack raised an inch or two from the burning sugar. Cover tightly, seal, and smoke for 25 or 30 minutes; or (2) Smoke a 1 pound fish on a rack in an oven-proof covered pot with live charcoal and pine needles or hickory wheels (soaked in water for a few hours) in an earthen barbecue pit for 30 minutes.

Five Spices *(wu hsiang)*. Available in powdered form already mixed. To prepare fresh, combine a little of each of the following in equal amounts: star aniseed, licorice root, cardamon, dried orange peel, and cinnamon. Place in a cloth bag.

garlic cloves, candied *(suan chan)*. Submerge garlic cloves in sugar for a few weeks, wash, cut, and serve.

ginger root, fresh *(sheng chiang)*. Substitute ¼ teaspoon ginger powder for 1 tablespoon chopped ginger root.

gingko nuts *(pai kuo)*. Parch for a few minutes and then shell.

green onion *(ta tsung)*. Use white part only.

green plums, sugared *(ch'ing mei)*. Canned.

green vegetables *(ch'ing ts'ai)*. Similar to fresh Western

soup greens. These contain starwort, celery, rape, etc.

haws, dried *(shan cha)*. Substitute fresh or dried crab apples.

jasmine, fresh *(mo li hua)*. Substitute honeysuckle.

Judas' ears, dried *(mo erh)*. Soak in water for 10 minutes, wash, and drain.

kelp, dried *(hai tai)*. This comes in 2′ sheets and makes wonderful bouillon.

lard *(huang yu)*. Only the fat surrounding the hog's heart was used in court dishes but other shortening may be substituted in equal quantities. It is either cubed or rendered.

laver, dried *(tzu ts'ai)*.

leek flower, salted *(yen chiu ts'ai)*. Let leek flowers stand in salt for a week, steep in hot water for a few minutes, and drain.

leek sprout, fresh *(chiu ts'ai miao)*.

licorice flowers, dried *(kan tsao hua)*. Soak in water for a few minutes, wash, and drain.

licorice root, dried *(kan tsao)*.

lily bulb, fresh *(bai ho ken)*.

lotus leaves, fresh in season *(he yeh)*. Substitute bamboo leaves or other large harmless leaves.

lotus root, fresh *(ou)*.

lotus seeds, dried *(lien tzu)*. Steep in hot water for 20 minutes, skin, and discard center.

lotus seeds, sugared *(lien tzu chan)*.

mandarin fish *(kuei yü)*. Porpoise, but any white flesh fish may be substituted.

marrow *(tung kua)*. This is vegetable marrow. Substitute any squash that can be stuffed.

mountain potatoes *(san yao)*. White potatoes may be substituted.

mushrooms, dried *(hsiang, ku, mo ku, kuo mo)*. Although these recipes originally required the now unavailable Mongolian mushrooms, Japanese dried mushrooms *(shiitake)* may be substituted.

orange peel, dried *(chen p'i)*.

peppercorn oil *(hua chiao yu)*. Fry ½ teaspoon peppercorns in 1 tablespoon sesame oil over medium heat until they are almost parched. Use oil only. Leftover oil may be kept for later use.

peppercorns, parched *(hung kan hua chiao)*. Parch in a frying pan over medium heat.

pine seeds or pine nuts *(sung tzu)*. Use shelled seeds only.

pork fat *(huang yu)*. Only the fat surrounding the hog's heart was used in court dishes but other shortening may be substituted in equal quantities. It is either cubed or rendered.

pork kidneys *(chu yao)*. Cut in half and remove center whites, wash, drain, and cut.

red pepper oil *(la yu)*. Simmer 5 or 6 red peppers in 1 cup sesame oil over low heat for 1 hour. Use oil only.

red pepper paste *(la chiang)*.

rice, cooked *(ta mi fan)*. To prepare rice: wash, rinse, and drain 1 cup rice, add 2 cups water and let stand for 10 minutes. Bring to a boil covered over high heat. Uncover and boil for 3 minutes. Reduce heat to low, cover, and let rice simmer for 10 minutes. Turn off heat and let covered rice stand for another 10 minutes. One cup raw rice produces 3 bowls cooked rice.

rice bran *(k'ang)*.

rice, glutinous *(lo mi)*.

rice powder, glutinous *(lo mi fen)*.

river fish *(lien yü)*. Similar to carp but any fresh water fish may be substituted.

rose essence *(mei kuei lu)*. This is a wine. Vanilla may be substituted.

scallops, dried *(kan shan ling)*. Steep in hot water for 20 minutes and drain.

sea cucumbers, dried *(hai shen)*. Soak in water for 3 days, changing the water each day. Boil 1 hour over medium heat, cut in halves, remove insides and discard. Wash thoroughly. Quarter and boil again until tender. The least bit of oil in the pot will prevent the sea cucumbers from becoming tender.

sesame oil *(tzu ma yu or hsiang yu)*.

sesame paste *(tzu ma chiang)*. Peanut butter may be substituted in equal quantities.

shark's fin, dried *(yü ch'ih)*. These are graded as dorsal, caudal, and pectoral. Regardless of type, all require boiling with an 8″ stalk of green onion and 1″ cube of ginger root per pound over medium heat until tender. Rinse many times and drain. The small type, pectoral *(ho sui ch'ih)*, come already processed and are known as golden fin *(jin ch'ih)* and require soaking overnight and boiling for 1 hour or more. The caudal *(chin wei, mao lo wei, chi chieh wei)* is the largest, being the tail, and requires soaking for 2 or 3 days, changing the water each day, and boiling many hours until tender. The dorsal *(pei ch'ih)*, the fin on the back, is also quite large and requires soaking for 2 or 3 days and the same processing as the caudal.

shrimp, dried *(hsia mi)*. Soak in hot water 15 minutes and drain.

shrimp sauce *(hsia mi yu)*.

soured Chinese cabbage *(suan pai ts'ai)*. Pickled and soured in brine. Sauerkraut may be substituted.

soy bean paste, sweet *(tien mien chiang)*.

soy beans, fresh *(ta tou)*. Substitute fresh peas.

squid, see cuttlefish.

star aniseed, dried *(pa chiao)*.

swallows' nests, dried *(yen ts'ai)*. Steep in hot water 4 hours, remove feathers carefully with forceps so as not to break the nests. Wrap nests carefully in a cloth bag, rinse many times, and drain.

Ten Spices *(ta liao)*. To prepare fresh, combine a little of each of the following in equal quantities and place in a cloth bag: star aniseed, dried orange peel, 1″ long cinnamon stick, ginger root, licorice root, cardamon, nutmeg, caraway, red pepper, and peppercorn.

tuberose, fresh *(yü chung pan)*. Check your florist. To use: remove pistils but take care not to break the shape of the corollas.

vegetable greens, pickled *(hsueh li hung)*.

vegetable greens, preserved with salt and dried *(mei kan ts'ai)*.

vegetable root, pickled *(cha ts'ai)*. Wash thoroughly before using.

vinegar, Chinese *(ts'u)*.

water chestnuts *(pi ch'i)*, canned or fresh.

water shields, fresh *(shun ts'ai)*. Substitute watercress or parsley.

watermelon seeds *(kua tzu)*.

wine lees *(jiu tsao)*. Available in powdered or cake form.

yellow wine *(huang jiu)*. Substitute sherry, cognac, or saké.

STOCK
FOR
COURT DISHES

CHICKEN STOCK

Chi T'ang

5 pounds stewing chicken, dressed
3 2"-pieces green onion
1/2" cube ginger
1/2 tablespoon licorice root (in a cloth bag)

Place the chicken in a pot and pour in twice as much water as the volume of the chicken. Add onion, ginger, and licorice. Bring to a boil uncovered over high heat, then reduce heat to low and simmer until the chicken becomes very tender. Chicken is discarded. Strain before using.

PORK STOCK

Pai T'ang or Kao T'ang

2 pounds pork butt
1 2"-piece green onion
½" cube ginger

Place the pork in a pot and pour in twice as much water as the volume of the pork. Add onion and ginger. Bring to a boil uncovered over high heat, then reduce the heat to low and simmer until the pork is very tender. Pork is discarded. Strain before using.

SPARERIB STOCK

Che Ku T'ang

4 pounds spareribs
2 2"-pieces green onion
½" cube ginger

Place the spareribs in a pot and pour in twice as much water as the volume of the spareribs. Add onion and ginger. Bring to a boil uncovered over high heat, then reduce heat to low and simmer for 1 hour or more. The spareribs are discarded. Strain before using.

CARP STOCK

Chi Yü T'ang

5 carp 6″ long
2 1″-pieces green onion
½″ cube ginger

Clean and wash the carp. Place in a pot and pour in twice as much water as the volume of the fish. Add onion and ginger. Bring to a boil uncovered over high heat for 20 minutes. Carp is discarded. Strain before using.

ABALONE STOCK

Pao Yü T'ang

1 pound dried abalone
3 1″-pieces green onion
¼″ cube ginger

Steep abalone in hot water for 30 minutes. Wash, place in a pot, and pour in five times as much water. Add onion and ginger. Bring to a boil uncovered over high heat, then reduce heat to low and simmer until the abalone becomes tender. Abalone is discarded. Strain before using.

VEGETABLE AND SEAFOOD STOCK

Shih Chin T'ang

10 pieces dried mushrooms (see page 36)
2 cups bean sprouts
1 carrot, quartered
2 2"-pieces green onion
1 pound Chinese cabbage
1 cup dried shrimp (see page 38)
5 dried scallops (see page 37)
1½" kelp

Place all ingredients in a large pot and pour in twice as much water as the volume of the ingredients. Bring to a boil uncovered over high heat, then reduce heat to low and simmer for 1½ hours or more. Ingredients are discarded. Strain before using.

CLEAR STOCK

Ch'ing T'ang

Add 2 egg shells to any thick stock. Let stand until stock becomes clear. Remove shells.

FISH
AND
SEA FOOD

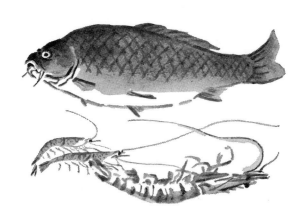

ABALONE AND ASPARAGUS WITH MILK

Nai Chih Erh Pai

3 abalone 3" diameter, canned, cut ¼" corrugated slices
20 asparagus stalks, canned
1 tablespoon chicken fat
1 cup milk or evaporated milk
1¼ teaspoon salt

Restore the sliced abalone to original shape, place them in a deep dish, and arrange asparagus stalks around them. Heat chicken fat, add milk and salt, and pour the mixture over the abalone and asparagus stalks. Steam 30 minutes. Serve hot. *Serves 3–4.*

BRAISED CARP

Hung Shao Li Yü

The following recipe was originated in Honan which is famous for delicious carp. In Honan everyday cooking, other vegetables, such as, carrots, string beans, and bean sprouts, are used.

2 pounds carp, scaled, insides removed, washed with salt water
    slashed 1/8" deep at an interval of 1" on both sides
3 tablespoons soy
1 teaspoon salt
1 tablespoon wine
½ tablespoon ginger root, julienned, and 1 piece ginger root in
    ½" cubes
2 cups and 2 tablespoons sesame oil
½ cup green onion, julienned
1 tablespoon sugar
1 cup water
½ cup dried mushrooms (see page 36), julienned
½ cup bamboo shoots (see page 33), julienned

Place the carp in a pan and marinate for 20 minutes with soy, ⅓ teaspoon salt, and wine, frequently basting. Save marinade. Rub the bottom of the pan with the cut end of the cubed ginger to prevent the fish from adhering to the bottom, then heat 2 cups sesame oil, bring to a boil over high heat, and fry the carp for 3 minutes. In another pan, bring 2 tablespoons sesame oil to a boil over high heat, then lower heat to medium and add ⅔ teaspoon salt, onion, and ginger root. Stir and add marinade, sugar, and water. Bring to a boil, add mushrooms and bamboo shoots, stir well, and put in the carp. Simmer uncovered over medium heat until hardly any liquid remains or about 30 minutes. When placing the carp on a platter, be very careful not to break its shape. Serve hot. *Serves 3–4.*

BRAISED SHARK'S FIN

Hung Shao Yü Ch'ih

2½ cups chicken stock (see page 41)
10 dried shrimp (see page 38)
2½ tablespoons peanut oil
¼ cup green onion, julienned, and 1 8" stalk
1 teaspoon ginger root, julienned, and 1 piece 1" cubed ginger
1 cup bamboo shoots (see page 33), julienned
4 pieces dried mushroom (see page 36), julienned
1 pound shark's fin (see page 38)
2 tablespoons wine
4 tablespoons soy
1 teaspoon salt
1 tablespoon cornstarch dissolved in ¼ cup water
1 teaspoon sesame oil

In a pot of chicken stock, add shrimp and bring to a boil. In another pan bring peanut oil to a boil over high heat and fry onion, ginger, bamboo, and mushrooms for 2 or 3 minutes, then add to the chicken stock. Add the shark's fin carefully to the stock and season with wine, soy, and salt. Lower heat to medium and simmer covered for 30 minutes. Add cornstarch paste. Reduce heat to very low and add sesame oil to enrich the flavor. Simmer, stirring constantly, until the liquid thickens. Serve hot. *Serves 5–6.*

CRAB AND SEA CUCUMBERS

Hsia Jou Hai Shen

4 tablespoons sesame oil
½ cup green onion, chopped
1¼ tablespoons ginger root, julienned
1½ cups bamboo shoots (see page 33), julienned
½ cup dried mushrooms (see page 36), julienned
1¼ cups crab meat, fresh or canned, bone removed
8 dried sea cucumbers (see page 37)
2 cups chicken stock (see page 41)
2 tablespoons wine
2 tablespoons soy
1½ teaspoons salt
½ teaspoon monosodium glutamate
2 tablespoons cornstarch dissolved in ½ cup water

Bring sesame oil to a boil in a pan over high heat and carefully fry onion and ginger. Add bamboo shoots, mushrooms, crab meat, and sea cucumber. Stir well and add the chicken stock. Bring to a boil, season with wine, soy, salt, and monosodium glutamate, and cook covered for 3 to 4 minutes. Add cornstarch paste and simmer uncovered, stirring constantly until the liquid thickens. Serve hot. *Serves 4–5.*

CRUCIAN CARP WITH RED PEPPER SAUCE

Chiang Pan Chi Yü

1½ pounds carp, scaled, cleaned, washed with salt water, and both sides scored

2 tablespoons cornstarch dissolved in ½ cup water

½ teaspoon salt or more to suit taste   } for marinade

1 tablespoon wine

1 teaspoon sesame oil

1" cube ginger root

1 quart sesame oil or enough to cover carp

½ cup pork, chopped

1 tablespoon ginger root, julienned

1 cup green onion, cut aslant in ½" pieces

2 tablespoons soy

2 cups chicken stock (see page 41)

1 tablespoon red pepper paste

2 tablespoons green soy beans, preferably fresh (if dried soy beans are used, soak them in water until softened before boiling)

Marinate the carp in marinade of cornstarch paste, salt, wine, and 1 teaspoon sesame oil for 30 minutes and baste frequently. Save the marinade. Heat an iron pan, rub the bottom with cut end of ginger root cube, and add 1 quart sesame oil. Bring to a boil over high heat and fry carp on both sides until brown. Strain and save oil for future use. Keep carp in warm place while preparing sauce. Using 2 tablespoons of strained oil, bring to a boil and add other ingredients. Temporarily transfer contents from the pan into a bowl. Place the carp in the same pan and pour both the sauce and marinade over it. Lower heat to medium, baste frequently, and simmer uncovered until liquid thickens. Serve hot. *Serves 3–4.*

CRUCIAN CARP SIMMERED IN VINEGAR SAUCE

Su Yü

Su Yü is a Shantung dish, and a most desirable dish to be served with wine.

10 carp $4\frac{1}{2}''$ long, scaled, insides removed, and washed with salt water
24 1"-long pieces green onion
4 tablespoons vinegar
6 tablespoons soy
1 tablespoon wine
1 teaspoon sesame oil
2 teaspoons sugar
1 tablespoon green tea, liquid
5 pieces ginger root in $\frac{1}{2}''$ cubes
2 licorice roots $\frac{3}{4}''$ long, placed in a cloth bag and tied with a string long enough to suspend into the pot

Use a medium sized earthen pot, if possible. Place a rack or dish at the bottom of the pot to prevent the fish from scorching. Arrange alternate layers of fish and onion and pour in the sauce made by mixing vinegar, soy, wine, sesame oil, sugar, tea, and ginger. Suspend the cloth bag of licorice in the pot and tie to the side. Fill the pot with water until it reaches $\frac{1}{2}''$ above the top layer. Cover with a lid, seal with paper, and simmer 5 to 6 hours over low fire or until the sound of simmering water ceases. The entire fish becomes tender including the bones, and even the head and tail are delicious. Serve cold. *Serves 3.*

DEEP-FRIED FISH

Chua Ch'ao Yü

This dish originated in Peking. Being far from a large river, Peking had to depend on Tientsin for her supply of fish and, at one time, was not too familiar with the art of cooking seafood. Therefore, it is interesting to note that the method of cooking meat is used in this recipe, but this dish is very flavorsome.

2 cups and 1 tablespoon sesame oil

1 pound any white flesh fish (such as flounder) scaled, insides removed, washed with salt water, and cut in 2" × 3" × ½" pieces

¼ teaspoon black pepper

1 egg, beaten

2 tablespoons cornstarch dissolved in ½ cup water

½ cup water

4 1"-long pieces green onion

1 teaspoon ginger root, chopped

4 tablespoons soy

Bring 2 cups of sesame oil to a boil in a big iron pan. After the slices of fish have been sprinkled with black pepper and dipped into a batter of egg and cornstarch paste, slip slices of fish into the oil, one at a time, and fry until brown. Heat 1 tablespoon oil in another pan and put in onion and ginger. Stir and add soy and ½ cup of water. Bring to a boil and put in fried slices of fish. Simmer until hardly any liquid remains. Serve hot. *Serves 2.*

FRIED AND SIMMERED CARP

Kan Shao Chi Yü

During the reign of Emperor Ch'ien-lung, a famous Soochow cook, Chen Tung Kuan, introduced the following dish to the imperial court.

1 pound carp, scaled, insides removed, washed with salt water, and scored on both sides

3 tablespoons soy

2 teaspoons sugar

2 tablespoons wine

6 tablespoons sesame oil

4 2"-long pieces green onion

½ tablespoon ginger root, chopped

1 tablespoon vinegar

1 tablespoon water

In a bowl marinate the carp in a sauce of 2 tablespoons soy, 1 teaspoon sugar and 1 tablespoon wine for 20 minutes and baste frequently. Save the marinade. Bring 5 tablespoons oil to a boil over high heat and put in the carp. Lower heat to medium and fry it until it becomes light brown. Remove from the pan. In the same pan fry the onions until they turn a light brown. In another pan, bring 1 tablespoon oil to a boil over medium heat and add ginger, 1 tablespoon soy, 1 teaspoon sugar, 1 tablespoon wine, vinegar, water, and the marinade. Bring to a boil and put in the carp. Cover the fish with fried onion. Reduce heat to low, and baste frequently with the sauce. Simmer uncovered until hardly any liquid remains. Serve hot. *Serves 2.*

FRIED FISH WITH WINE LEES AND CORNSTARCH

Tsao Liu Yü Pien

This well known Shantung dish was added to the list of imperial recipes during the Ming period.

1 cup water
½ tablespoon green onion, chopped
½ teaspoon ginger root, chopped
1 tablespoon wine lees
1 teaspoon rice bran
1 teaspoon salt
2½ tablespoons cornstarch
3 tablespoons sesame oil
1 mandarin fish (see page 36), 15"-length, scaled, cleaned, washed with salt water, boned, and sliced aslant into ½" thickness (Substitute a 1½ pound white flesh fish.)

Combine in a bowl of water, onion, ginger, wine lees, rice bran, salt, and 1½ tablespoons cornstarch, and mix well. Dust fish with 1 tablespoon of cornstarch. Bring sesame oil to a boil in a pan over high heat. Remove the pan from the fire. Put slices of fish in the pan, replace the pan over the fire, lower heat to medium and fry until brown. Then add the combined ingredients, stirring gently, and simmer uncovered for a few minutes until the liquid thickens. Serve hot. *Serves 3.*

FRIED PRAWNS

Shao Ming Hsia

In March and April large quantities of prawns arrive on the market in Tientsin. The following dish is the original Tientsin style of cooking prawns. Nowadays, people like to use tomato sauce over prawns.

2 cups sesame oil
10 fresh prawns 4" to 6" long, shelled, deveined, and washed
½ cup green onion, julienned
1 teaspoon ginger root, chopped
1 ½ tablespoons soy
½ teaspoon garlic, chopped
1 tablespoon wine
½ teaspoon monosodium glutamate

Bring sesame oil to a boil in a pan and fry prawns for 1 minute. Remove from pan. Leave 2 tablespoons sesame oil in the pan, fry onion and ginger, stir, and add soy, prawns, garlic, wine, and monosodium glutamate. Fry, stirring briskly, for 2 or more minutes over high heat. Serve hot. *Serves 2–3.*

FRIED RIVER FISH

Wa Kuai Yü

When Emperor K'ang-hsi inspected the construction works on the Yellow River, he was served this Honan dish. He became very fond of it and, upon his return to Peking, he ordered it to be entered in the list of imperial recipes.

1 teaspoon sesame oil
2 tablespoons green onion, chopped
1 tablespoon ginger root, chopped
1 tablespoon soy
1 tablespoon vinegar
1 tablespoon sugar
1 tablespoon wine
1 tablespoon water
2 tablespoons cornstarch dissolved in ½ cup water
Salt to suit taste
1 pound sesame oil for frying
1 pound river fish (trout or similar), scaled, cleaned, washed in salt water, and cut aslant ¼" slices.

Prepare a sauce by heating 1 teaspoon oil in a pan over medium heat and frying onion and ginger. Add soy, vinegar, sugar, wine, and water. Stir well and bring to a boil. Taste and, if necessary, add salt. Add cornstarch paste, simmer, stirring constantly, until the liquid thickens and keep the sauce warm in a double boiler. Bring sesame oil to a boil in a large pan over high heat. Remove the pan from the fire and put in the slices of fish. Replace the pan on the fire and bring to a boil over high heat. Thus alternate heating and cooling so that the fish will become a light brown without overcooking or undercooking. Pour the sauce over the slices of fish on a dish. See note at bottom of next page. Serve hot. *Serves 2.*

FRIED SHRIMP

Ch'ing Ch'ao Hsia Jen

Ch'ing Ch'ao Hsia Jen is a noted dish of the district along the lower Yangtze. It was introduced to the court during Emperor Yung-cheng's reign (1723–1735) and was highly appreciated by the emperors who followed.

6 tablespoons sesame oil
1 tablespoon ginger root, chopped
2 tablespoons green onion, chopped
1 pound fresh shrimp 2" long, shelled, deveined, washed, and dredged in cornstarch
5 tablespoons wine
1 teaspoon salt

Bring the sesame oil to a boil in an iron pan over high heat. Remove from the fire, put in ginger and onion, and stir. Replace the pan over the fire, add shrimp, wine, and salt, and fry, stirring briskly, for a few minutes. Serve hot. *Serves 2.*

(Continued from page fifty-six)
NOTE: In the olden days it was not possible to adjust the heat, which is the reason for the above method. Now there is no need to remove the pan from the stove.

FRIED SMOKED FISH

Hsün Yü (Cha)

3 tablespoons sesame oil
1 tablespoon green onion, chopped
2 teaspoons ginger root, chopped
½ teaspoon Five Spices (see page 35)
2 smoked fish (trout or flounder), 10" long cut in 1" pieces
   (see page 35)
½ cup chicken stock (see page 41)
2 tablespoons soy
1 tablespoon wine
½ tablespoon sugar
2 tablespoons cornstarch dissolved in 1 cup water

Bring the sesame oil to a boil in a pan over high heat and add onion, ginger, Five Spices, smoked fish, and chicken stock. Bring to a boil. Season with soy, wine, and sugar and cook 1 minute. Lower temperature and add cornstarch paste. Simmer uncovered, stirring frequently, until hardly any liquid remains. Serve hot. *Serves 3–4.*

PRAWNS AND PORK KIDNEYS WITH SOY

Pan Hsia Yao

1 ½ pounds prawns, shelled, deveined, washed, and cut in 2″
    lengths
3 pork kidneys (see page 37)
2 tablespoons sesame oil
10 peppercorns
2 tablespoons green onion, chopped
1 ½ teaspoons ginger root, chopped
7 tablespoons soy
2 tablespoons vinegar

Pour hot water over prawns until they are parboiled and over kidney slices until they are white. Arrange on a platter. Bring sesame oil to a boil in a pan, parch peppercorns, add other ingredients and mix well. Pour sauce over prawns and kidneys. Serve hot. If desired, simmer prawns and kidneys in the sauce over moderate heat for a few minutes. *Serves 4–5.*

STEAMED CARP

Ch'ing Cheng Li Yü

The Yellow River which runs through the Honan Province produces the most delicious carp in all China. The following Honan recipe was entered in the list of imperial recipes.

1½ *pounds carp, scaled, insides removed, washed with salt water, and scored on both sides*
1½ *tablespoons pork fat in ½" cubes*
½ *cup green onion, julienned*
1 *tablespoon ginger root, julienned*
2 *tablespoons wine*
½ *teaspoon sugar*
1½ *teaspoons salt*
½ *cup water*

Place the carp in a deep dish, dot back and insides of the fish with fat cubes, and arrange onion and ginger around the carp. Pour over the carp a mixture of wine, sugar, salt, and water. Steam for 30 minutes. Do not oversteam. (If a vinegar and ginger sauce is desired, to 3 tablespoons vinegar add 1 teaspoon ginger root, chopped.) Serve hot. *Serves 2–3.*

STEAMED FLOUNDER

Ch'ing Cheng Pi Mu Yü

1 flounder 15" length, scaled, cleaned, washed with salt water
   and scored
2 tablespoons pork fat, cubed in $\frac{1}{2}$" pieces
1 tablespoon green onion, chopped
2 tablespoons ginger root, julienned
1 teaspoon salt
2 tablespoons wine
$\frac{1}{2}$ teaspoon cardamom
1 cup fish stock (see page 43)

Place the fish in a dish of medium depth, dot with pork
fat, and sprinkle with onion, ginger, salt, wine, and
cardamom. Pour in fish stock and steam for 40 minutes.
Serve hot. Oversteaming will spoil the flavor. *Serves 3.*

STEWED CRAB MEAT

Hui Hsia Jou

5 tablespoons lard
16 1" long pieces green onion
1/4 cup ginger root, julienned
4 cups crab meat, fresh or canned, bones removed
2 cups chicken stock
1/2 cup soy
1 teaspoon vinegar
3 tablespoons wine
1 tablespoon sugar
1 teaspoon monosodium glutamate
3 tablespoons cornstarch dissolved in 5 tablespoons water

Heat lard in a pan and add all ingredients. Stir gently and simmer over moderate temperature until the liquid thickens. Serve hot. When crabs have an abundance of spawns, this dish is especially delicious. *Serves 4–5.*

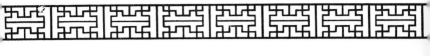

CHICKEN
AND
DUCK

BEGGARS' CHICKEN

Hua Tzu Chi

Among the beggars in northern China there were once chicken thieves who would steal chickens to sell or to eat themselves. Having no proper utensils for cooking or not knowing anyone from whom to borrow them, they killed the chickens and cooked them by the river as in the recipe below, although they used only soy for stuffing and driftwood for fuel instead of charcoal. The beggar buried his chicken in a hole filled with hot coals and covered the hole with sand or soil. He then stuck crossed twigs in the mound as a mark of ownership. In the meantime, while the chicken was cooking, he would forage for other things to steal or beg. If another beggar happened to find the mound, he also placed crossed twigs on it, thus claiming the right to be given a share and join in the feast when the chicken was ready. This bears out the old adage, "There is honor even among thieves."

During the uprising of the Boxers in 1900, Empress Dowager Tzu-hsi, who had escaped from Peking, stopped in the Huai Lai district. This unexpected visit of the sovereign embarrassed the district governor who did not know what to serve her for dinner as Huai Lai was a very poor area. Fortunately, there was among the followers of the empress dowager a eunuch from this district who described "Beggars' Chicken." The empress dowager ordered a chicken to be cooked in this fashion. She so enjoyed this dish that she had it included in the list of court dishes.

5½ pounds fat hen with feathers. Remove intestines, head, and
   feet, but do not pluck the feathers. Wash inside of the chicken
   thoroughly
8 1″ long pieces green onion
1″ cubed ginger root, crushed
1 teaspoon sugar
4 tablespoons soy
1 teaspoon wine
1 tablespoon flour
1 tablespoon water
1 needle threaded with a 20″ thread
Potters' clay

Stuff the chicken with a mixture of onion, ginger, sugar,
soy and wine. Sew and seal stitched area with a paste
prepared from flour and water. Then cover the entire
chicken with 2″ thickness of clay. Dig a hole 2′ × 2′ × 2′
in the ground and fill it with burning charcoal, broken
in pieces, to 16″ in depth. Bury the chicken in the charcoal and cover with sand or soil. Cook for two hours
until a sizzling sound is heard from the lump of clay.
Remove with a shovel and wait until the clay is cool
enough to handle. With a chopper cut all around the
hardened clay lump and break open with hands. The
feathers and skin adhere to the clay. Remove chicken
meat with chopsticks and serve on a plate. Serve hot. A
chicken prepared in the above manner is both tender and
unusually moist. One cup cooked rice added to the
stuffing is delicious. *Serves 7–8*.

CHICKEN AND BEAN CURD SKIN

Tou Szu Kuo Shao Chi

In March 1784 when Emperor Chi'en-lung made an inspection tour to the South and stopped in An Lan Yuan, Hainan, he enjoyed *Tou Szu Kuo Shao Chi* offered by Chen Yuan Lung. Upon his return to Peking, he ordered this dish to be entered in the list of imperial recipes.

5 pounds fat chicken, dressed
3 tablespoons soy
1 tablespoon wine
1 4″ piece green onion and 2 tablespoons chopped green onion
1½ tablespoons ginger root, sliced
3 tablespoons sesame oil
¼ pound bean curd skin, julienned
¼ cup water
1 tablespoon salt or more to suit taste
½ teaspoon sugar

Put chicken in an earthen pot 8″ deep and 12″ diameter, pour in enough water to submerge half of the chicken, add 1⅔ tablespoons soy, wine, green onion pieces, 1 tablespoon ginger slices, and cook covered over moderate heat for 40 minutes. Drain well and julienne boiled chicken meat. Bring sesame oil to a boil in a pan. Add chopped onion and ½ tablespoon ginger slices. Stir. Add 1⅓ tablespoons soy and bring to a boil. Add bean curd skin, fry 2 minutes, and then add chicken meat, water, salt, and sugar. Simmer uncovered until hardly any liquid remains. Serve hot. *Serves 5–6.*

CHICKEN AND SHRIMP

Chi Ting Hsia Jen

This Soochow dish was greatly enjoyed by Emperor Ch'ien-lung during his inspection tour in southern China. Upon his return to Peking, he ordered this recipe to be entered in the list of imperial recipes.

2 tablespoons sesame oil
½ pound chicken meat, in ½" cubes
1½ tablespoons cornstarch
1 pound shrimp, shelled and deveined, and cut in 2" lengths
2 teaspoons green onion, chopped
1 teaspoon ginger root, chopped
2 tablespoons soy
1 teaspoon salt or more to suit taste
3 tablespoons wine
½ teaspoon sugar

Bring sesame oil to a boil in a pan, add chicken meat dredged with cornstarch, and fry 5 seconds over high heat. Add shrimp and fry together, stirring constantly for 2 or 3 minutes. Add rest of the ingredients, stir well, and bring almost to a boil. Serve hot. *Serves 3–4.*

CHICKEN COOKED WITH BEAN CURD

Chi P'ien Shao Tou Fu

Chi P'ien Shao Tou Fu was devised in Peking. In the cooking of ordinary citizens additional ingredients were used.

5 pounds chicken, dressed
2 2½" long pieces green onion and 1 tablespoon, chopped
2 pieces ginger root: one 1" cube, and one 1" cube cut in half
1 tablespoon salt or more if necessary
2 cups and 1 tablespoon sesame oil
1¼ pounds bean curd, cut 1" × ½" × ½"
4 tablespoons soy
1 cup chicken stock (see page 41)

Place the chicken in a large pot and fill with enough water to cover the chicken. Put in 2 pieces of green onion, 1" ginger cube, and 1 teaspoon salt, and cook over high heat for 40 minutes uncovered. Remove the chicken from the pot and keep the stock for later use. Julienne boiled chicken meat into 2" slivers. Bring 2 cups of sesame oil to a boil in a pan, fry the bean curd until light brown and drain. Heat 1 tablespoon oil in another pan, put in 1 tablespoon chopped onion and 2 halves of ginger cube and stir. Add soy and bring to a boil. Pour in chicken stock, add chicken meat and fried bean curd and 2 teaspoons salt. Simmer uncovered over low heat until hardly any liquid remains. Serve hot. *Serves 6–7.*

FIVE SPICES CHICKEN

Wu Hsiang Chi

This seasonal dish for fall was originally a Chiangnan dish
called *Wu Su Chi* and was later renamed *Wu Hsiang Chi* in
the imperial court.

5 pounds fat hen, dressed
1 ½ teaspoons Five Spices (see page 35)
5 tablespoons salt
2 tablespoons soy
½ teaspoon sugar
2 quarts and 2 tablespoons sesame oil
1 tablespoon wine
2 teaspoons peppercorns, parched and crushed (see page 37)

Fill a large pot ⅔ full of water, bring to a boil and then
lower heat. Put in 1 teaspoon Five Spices, 1 tablespoon
salt, and the chicken. Simmer over low heat for 1 hour
covered. In the meantime, prepare a sauce of ½ teaspoon
Five Spices, 2 tablespoons salt, soy, sugar, 2 tablespoons
sesame oil, and wine in a bowl. After the chicken has
been boiled and while it is still hot, place it on a large
plate and brush the sauce over the entire surface of the
chicken until it turns a light brownish color. Place the
chicken in a well ventilated place to dry. Bring to a boil
2 quarts sesame oil in a deep pan over high heat, and fry
the chicken until it turns almost reddish. Cut in bite-size
pieces. Serve with a saucer containing 2 tablespoons of
salt and 2 teaspoons of parched peppercorns to season.
Serve hot. *Serves 5–6.*

FRIED CHICKEN CUBES

Kun Pao Chi Ting

During the time Lord Li Hung Chang was the Minister of Naval, Military, and Diplomatic Affairs of Northern China, he enjoyed this dish very much. Later, it was introduced to the imperial court. Lord Li Hung Chang was the first ambassador to the United States from Imperial China.

½ *pound chicken meat, in ¼″ cubes*
¼ *teaspoon black pepper*
¼ *cup cornstarch*
2 *teaspoons green onion, chopped*
1 *teaspoon ginger root, chopped*
4 *tablespoons sesame oil*
1 *red pepper, seeds removed, and julienned*
3 *tablespoons soy*
2 *teaspoons sugar*
1 *tablespoon wine*

Sprinkle chicken cubes with black pepper and dredge with cornstarch. Add 1 teaspoon onion and ½ teaspoon ginger root and mix well. Bring 3 tablespoons sesame oil to a boil in a pan over high heat. Fry chicken cubes, stirring briskly, for 2 minutes and remove from the pan. Heat 1 tablespoon sesame oil in another pan over high heat. Fry red pepper until slightly burnt, add 1 teaspoon onion, ½ teaspoon ginger, soy, sugar, and wine. Bring to a boil and add the fried chicken cubes. Fry, stirring constantly, for 1 to 2 minutes. Serve hot. *Serves 2*.

FRIED CHICKEN FILLETS WITH EGG WHITE

Hui Chi Yung

5 chicken fillets, pounded thin with the back of a chopper
1 egg white
1 tablespoon cornstarch
2 tablespoons sesame oil
½ teaspoon ginger root, chopped
½ teaspoon green onion, chopped
2 tablespoons wine
4 tablespoons water
1 teaspoon salt
1 teaspoon sugar
3 beefsteak plant or lettuce leaves (see page 34), shredded

Dip chicken fillets in a mixture of egg white and corn-starch. Bring sesame oil to a boil in a pan and fry chicken a few minutes. Add sauce of ginger, onion, wine, water, salt, and sugar. When thickened, add beefsteak plant or lettuce leaves, and cook for a few seconds. Serve immediately. Serve hot. *Serves 2.*

FRIED CHICKEN GIBLETS

Ch'ao Shih Chien

This recipe was prepared in the court as shown below, but the amount and kinds of ingredients varied in the popular versions of the ordinary citizens.

½ pound chicken giblets, julienned
2 tablespoons sesame oil
½ cup green onion, julienned
2 teaspoons ginger root, julienned
2 tablespoons soy
¼ teaspoon salt
½ teaspoon monosodium glutamate
½ cup bamboo shoots (see page 33), julienned
3 tablespoons wine

To extract odor and to tenderize the giblets, place them in a sieve and pour hot water over them until whitened. Bring sesame oil to a boil in a pan over high heat, add onion, ginger, soy, salt, and monosodium glutamate and stir. Bring to a boil and add bamboo shoots and wine. Bring to a boil and add giblets. Fry, stirring briskly, over high heat, for a few minutes. Serve hot. *Serves 2–3.*

Celadon basin, made to order by the imperial kiln, Southern Sung Dynasty, 1127–1279

Porcelain dish, from Chia Ching, Ming Dynasty, 1522–1567

Porcelain bowls, from Wan Li, Ming Dynasty, 1573–1621

Porcelain bowls, from Kang Hsi, Ching Dynasty, 1662–1723

Above: Porcelain bowl and dish. At right: Celadon and porcelain bowls. All from Yung Cheng, Ching Dynasty, 1723–1736.

From Chien Lung, Ching Dynasty, 1736–1796

From Chien Lung, Ching Dynasty, 1736–1796

Porcelain wine bottle, from Chia Ching, Ming Dynasty, 1522–1567. The basic color is white, with the design executed in red, green, blue, yellow and black. The carved section was first painted yellow and then covered with gold. This bottle, made at a kiln in the province of Chianghsi, is considered to be a foremost example of China's famous gold-painted porcelain, of which there remain but very few examples in the world. This one has been officially designated as a Japanese national treasure. *Page eighty*

FRIED CHICKEN WITH EGG WHITES

Fu Yung Chi Szu

In *Tung Ching Men Hua Lu,* one of the earliest publications in China containing reminiscences of the life in northern Sung court by the refugees of the southern Sung, is found the recipe for this Shantung dish.

3 egg whites
2 tablespoons water
2 tablespoons cornstarch
2 tablespoons green onion, julienned
1 teaspoon ginger root, julienned
1 teaspoon salt
1 teaspoon sugar
1 tablespoon wine
3 tablespoons sesame oil
⅔ pound chicken meat, julienned

Combine the following ingredients in a bowl and mix well: egg whites, water, 1 teaspoon cornstarch, onion, ginger, salt, sugar and wine. Dust chicken with 1⅔ tablespoons cornstarch. Bring sesame oil to a boil and remove pan from fire. Put chicken meat into the pan and fry with the heat of the pan, stirring constantly, until the meat turns white. Replace pan over fire and add the combined ingredients, simmer, while stirring, for a few minutes. Serve hot. Do not overcook the chicken. *Serves 2.*

FRIED CHICKEN WITH PEPPERCORNS

Cha Pa Kuai

Late in the Ming Period, this Shantung dish was introduced to the imperial court.

2 fryers, 1 pound each, dressed, legs and wings removed, bodies
  cut in four pieces
3 tablespoons soy
2 1" long pieces green onion
1" cube ginger root, quartered
10 peppercorns, parched and crushed (see page 37)
1 teaspoon salt
2 eggs
4 tablespoons cornstarch
1 cup water
3 cups sesame oil

In a bowl combine soy, onion, and ginger and mix well. Marinate the chicken pieces for 20 minutes and drain. Break eggs into a bowl, add cornstarch and water and mix well into a batter. Bring sesame oil to a boil over high heat in a large pan. Put in pieces of chicken dipped in the batter. Fry until light brown. Serve hot sprinkled with peppercorns mixed with salt. *Serves 2–3.*

FRIED CHICKEN GIZZARD WITH WALNUTS

Cha Cher

3⁄4 *pound gizzards, insides removed, washed, drained, and*
  quartered (I prefer julienned.)
5 *tablespoons soy*
2 *teaspoons ginger root, julienned*
4 *tablespoons green onion, julienned*
2 *tablespoons wine*
5 *tablespoons sesame oil*
1 *cup walnut meats, blanched*

Marinate gizzards in a marinade of soy, ginger, onion,
and wine. Bring to a boil 4 tablespoons sesame oil and fry
gizzards quickly for a minute or so over high heat. Bring
to a boil 1 tablespoon sesame oil in another pan and sauté
walnuts until crisp. Arrange gizzards and walnut meats
side by side on a plate and serve. Serve hot. *Serves 2–3.*

FRIED JULIENNED CHICKEN MEAT

Ch'ing Ch'ao Chi P'ien

This Chiangnan dish is light in flavor and it is ideal for summer.

2 tablespoons sesame oil
½ pound chicken meat, julienned
2 tablespoons cornstarch
1 teaspoon green onion, chopped
½ teaspoon ginger root, chopped
½ teaspoon garlic, chopped
1 tablespoon wine
½ teaspoon salt
1 piece coriander or lettuce, julienned

Bring the sesame oil to a boil in a pan over high heat. Put in the chicken meat dredged with cornstarch and stir. Add onion, ginger, and garlic and stir. Then add wine, salt, and coriander and stir briskly for a few seconds. Serve hot. Do not overcook chicken and coriander. *Serves 1–2.*

SHREDDED CHICKEN

Pai Ch'ieh Chi

Although time-consuming, a chicken cooked in the ancient manner as below has a different flavor from one steamed or boiled.

3 pound broiler, dressed
3 tablespoons soy
1 ½ tablespoons vinegar
1 tablespoon sesame oil

Boil water in a large pot and place a bar a foot above the caldron. At the center of the bar, fasten the chicken. Ladle boiling water over the chicken for 2 hours. With fingers shred the boiled white meat of the chicken. Arrange shreds on a plate and serve with a sauce of soy, vinegar, and sesame oil. Serve cold or hot. *Serves 3–4.*

SHREDDED CHICKEN WITH SAUCE

Kuai Wei Chi

2 pounds chicken, shredded. Cook chicken as in recipe for Shredded Chicken. If too time-consuming, boil chicken meat and shred.

¼ cup green onion, chopped

1 teaspoon ginger root, chopped

5 teaspoons fermented bean curd, spiced variety (chiang tou fu)

2 tablespoons sesame paste

½ tablespoon mustard

½ cup soy

2 tablespoons sesame oil

½ teaspoon monosodium glutamate

Prepare a sauce by combining the following ingredients: onion, ginger, fermented bean curd, sesame paste, mustard, soy, sesame oil, and monosodium glutamate, and mix well. Serve shredded chicken with the sauce. Serve hot or cold. *Serves 2.*

SMOKED AND FRESH CHICKEN JULIENNED

Hui Liang Chi Szu

3 tablespoons sesame oil
½ cup green onion, julienned
½ cup bamboo shoots (see page 33), julienned
½ pound smoked chicken, julienned (see page 34)
½ pound fresh chicken, julienned
2 cups chicken stock (see page 41)
1 teaspoon salt
½ teaspoon monosodium glutamate

Bring sesame oil to a boil in a pan, add onion and bamboo shoots and fry, stirring constantly, over high heat for 2 minutes. Add smoked and fresh chicken and chicken stock, stir well and bring to a boil. Simmer uncovered for 2 to 3 minutes until the fresh chicken is done. Season with salt and monosodium glutamate. Serve hot. Do not substitute roasted chicken for smoked chicken. *Serves 3–4.*

SMOKED CHICKEN WITH CHINESE CABBAGE

Fei Chi Huo Yen Hsün Pai Ts'ai

This famous Soochow dish was introduced to the imperial court by Chen Tung Kuan who was cook for the Chen family in Soochow. Emperor Ch'ien-Lung praised the cook so highly that the master of the Chen family gave the cook to the emperor, who accompanied his highness to Peking and served his highness for many years. The Emperor loved rich food and this was one of his favorites.

4 pounds fat chicken, bound tightly with a string, parboiled, and smoked (see page 34)

3 tablespoons soy

4 tablespoons wine

1½ tablespoons sugar

1 teaspoon peppercorns

1 teaspoon Ten Spices (see page 38)

6 tablespoons lard

4 pounds Chinese cabbage, julienned in 4½" strips

2 tablespoons sesame oil

4 tablespoons green onion, chopped

2 tablespoons ginger root, quartered

½ cup water

1 tablespoon salt or more to suit taste

½ teaspoon monosodium glutamate

Place the chicken in a pot, pour in enough water to submerge half of the chicken, add 2 tablespoons soy, 1 tablespoon wine, 1 tablespoon sugar, peppercorns, and Ten Spices. Parboil for 30 minutes, basting frequently.

(Continued at bottom of next page)

STEAMED CHICKEN

Ch'ing Cheng Chi

This Shantung dish was very popular in the court.

5 pounds chicken, dressed
3 cups water
1 teaspoon lard
1 cup 1" long pieces green onion
2 tablespoons ginger root, chopped
1 dried licorice root
1 cup bamboo shoots (see page 33), julienned
4 dried mushrooms (see page 36), julienned
1½ tablespoons salt or more if necessary
1 teaspoon monosodium glutamate

Fill a large pot two thirds full of water and bring to a boil over high heat. Parboil chicken for 10 minutes, then place it in a large bowl. Pour in 3 cups of water and add other ingredients. Place the bowl in a steamer and steam over high heat for 2 hours. Serve hot. *Serves 6–7.*

(Continued from previous page)

After smoking bone the chicken and julienne the meat. Melt the lard in a large pan and fry cabbage strips until yellowish in color. Bring sesame oil to a boil in another iron pan, add green onion, ginger, 1 tablespoon soy, 3 tablespoons wine, 1½ tablespoons sugar, water, salt, and monosodium glutamate. Add smoked chicken and fried Chinese cabbage and stir well. Simmer uncovered until hardly any liquid remains. Serve hot or cold. *Serves 4–5.*

STEAMED DUCK WITH MUSHROOMS

Ch'ing Cheng Kou Mo Ya

5 pounds duck, dressed
8 1" long pieces green onion
1 tablespoon sliced ginger root
1 tablespoon salt or more to suit taste
1 cup dried mushrooms (see page 36), quartered
½ teaspoon monosodium glutamate
2 tablespoons wine

Place the duck in a large pot, preferably earthenware, with the breast down, and fill the pot with enough water to submerge the duck. Add other ingredients and then place in a steamer. Steam over high heat for 2 hours. Serve hot. *Serves 5–6.*

STEWED CHICKEN

Huang Men Chi Kuai

This Shantung dish is quite savory. It is mentioned in the original recipe that the longer the chicken is simmered, the better the flavor.

1 tablespoon sesame oil
¾ cup ¼" long pieces green onion
1" cubed ginger root, quartered
3 tablespoons soy
1 tablespoon salt
4 cups water
5 pounds chicken, cubed in 1" pieces including bones
1 teaspoon monosodium glutamate

Bring sesame oil to a boil in a pan over medium heat, put in onion and ginger and stir. Add soy and salt and bring to a boil. Add water and bring to a boil. Put in chicken cubes and sprinkle with monosodium glutamate. Reduce heat to low and simmer covered for 2 hours. Serve hot. *Serves 6–7.*

WALNUTS AND CHICKEN CUBES

He-t'ou Chi Ting

Chen Tung Kuan, the famous Soochow cook, introduced the following dish to the imperial court during the reign of Emperor Chi'en-lung.

4 tablespoons sesame oil
6 walnuts, blanched and quartered
⅔ pound chicken meat, in ½" cubes
1 tablespoon cornstarch
½ tablespoon green onion, chopped
1 teaspoon ginger root, chopped
2 tablespoons soy
1 tablespoon wine
1 teaspoon sugar
½ teaspoon salt

Bring sesame oil to a boil in a pan, fry walnut meats for 1 minute and remove. Put chicken dusted with cornstarch in same pan and fry over high heat for 2 minutes or more, stirring constantly, then add onion and ginger. Stir and add other ingredients. Fry, stirring briskly, for another minute. Serve hot. The combination of walnuts and chicken is most delicious. *Serves 2.*

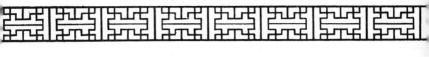

MEAT

BOILED AND STEAMED MUTTON WITH SAUCE

P'a Yang Jou

This Manchurian dish was a favorite of Emperor Ch'ien-lung. To serve the food hot, a special two-part dish was devised, containing hot water underneath and the food above.

6 pounds mutton loin
2 tablespoons green onion, chopped
2 tablespoons ginger root, chopped
1½ teaspoons peppercorns
1½ tablespoons salt or more to suit taste
3 tablespoons wine
4 tablespoons soy
1 tablespoon sugar
¼ cup chicken stock (see page 41)
1 teaspoon sesame oil

Place mutton in a pot with enough water to cover and add 1 tablespoon onion, 1 tablespoon ginger, 1 teaspoon peppercorns, and 1½ tablespoons salt. Bring to a boil over high heat, then reduce heat to low and simmer uncovered. Remove scum from the surface. When the liquid has been reduced to ⅓ of its original volume, add 3 tablespoons wine and 3 tablespoons soy and continue boiling until the mutton becomes tender and hardly any liquid remains. Do not cook the mutton until it becomes so tender that it is difficult to slice. Cut mutton in ¼" × 2" × 3" slices and arrange attractively in a bowl. Combine 1 tablespoon soy, 1 tablespoon onion, 1 tablespoon ginger, ½ teaspoon peppercorns, 1 tablespoon sugar, and chicken stock and pour the sauce over the

(Continued at bottom of next page)

BOILED MUTTON

Ma La Yang Jou

It is believed that this dish was brought to China by Moslems. However there is no mention in the list of imperial recipes as to when it was introduced.

$3\frac{1}{3}$ pounds mutton, in $1\frac{1}{2}''$ cubes
3 $1\frac{1}{2}''$ long pieces green onion
2 ginger root slices $1'' \times 1'' \times \frac{1}{8}''$ and $1\frac{1}{2}$ tablespoons ginger root, chopped
$\frac{3}{4}$ cup soy
1 tablespoon wine
1 teaspoon sesame oil
1 teaspoon peppercorns, parched and ground fine (see page 37)

Place mutton cubes in a pot, pour in enough water to cover, and add onion and ginger slices. Boil over low heat uncovered until the water has been reduced to half its volume. Remove white scum from the surface whenever it appears. Add soy and wine and keep cooking until no liquid remains. Add sesame oil, chopped ginger, and ground peppercorns. Mix well with mutton. This dish is served cold, but it is also tasty when it is hot. Cook the meat just long enough to retain shape of the cubes. *Serves 6–7.*

(Continued from previous page)
mutton slices. Steam the bowl of mutton over high heat for 20 minutes until it becomes thoroughly tender. After removing the mutton slices carefully from the bowl into a deep dish, add 1 teaspoon sesame oil for flavoring. Sauce may be poured over or served individually. Serve hot. *Serves 10–12.*

BRAISED HEAD OF "TIGER"

Hung Shao Shih Tzu T'ou

Hung Shao Shih Tzu Tou is a famous Chiangnan dish and was introduced to the imperial court during the reign of Emperor Ch'ien-lung.

½ *pound lean pork, tendons removed, chopped*

½ *pound fat pork, tendons removed, chopped*

1½ *egg whites*

2 *tablespoons cornstarch*

1 *teaspoon salt*

2½ *cups sesame oil*

4 ½" *long pieces green onion*

½" *cube ginger root, crushed*

2 *cups bamboo shoots, julienned*

2 *tablespoons soy*

1 *tablespoon wine*

1 *teaspoon sugar*

1 *cup water*

Put in a bowl the chopped pork, egg whites, cornstarch, and salt and mix well. Form pork into balls of 2″ diameter. Bring sesame oil to a boil in a pan and fry meat balls until browned. Place them in a bowl, add onion and ginger, and sprinkle slivers of bamboo shoots over the meat balls. Make a sauce of soy, wine, sugar, and water and pour over the pork balls. Steam for 1 hour at high heat. Serve hot. *Serves 3–4.*

BRAISED PORK AND CHINESE CABBAGE

Hung Shao Jou

In this Chiangnan dish, sweet potatoes or Irish potatoes were used by ordinary citizens, but in the court only Chinese cabbage was used in the winter and spinach in the summer.

1 pound fresh bacon with skin
1 2" long piece green onion plus 2 tablespoons green onion, chopped
2 pieces ginger root in ¾" cubes, crushed
1 teaspoon peppercorns
4 tablespoons soy
1 teaspoon sugar
1 tablespoon wine
¼ pound Chinese cabbage, cut aslant

Fill a medium sized pot half full of water and put in the whole piece of bacon, green onion stalk, 1 piece ginger, and peppercorns. Cook 1 hour over moderate heat covered. Remove meat from the pot and cut in 1½" cubes. Place cubes in a bowl, add soy, sugar, wine, chopped onion, and 1 piece ginger. Mix well and marinate for 20 minutes. Rearrange cubes in the bowl with the skin side up. Cover with half the marinade, arrange Chinese cabbage on the cubes, and pour the rest of the marinade over the cabbage. Steam for 1 hour. Serve hot. *Serves 2–3.*

BRAISED SMOKED HAM

Hung Men Chou Tzu

6 pounds Chinese ham
4 1″ long pieces green onion
2 pieces ginger root in 1″ cubes, crushed
1 cup soy
4 tablespoons sugar
½ cup wine
1½ 1″ long pieces dried orange peel
2 to 3 star aniseeds
½ teaspoon Five Spices (see page 35)   *Placed in a cloth bag*
10 peppercorns

Fill a pot with enough water to cover the ham, add ginger and onion and bring to a boil over high heat. Lower to moderate heat and add soy, sugar, wine, and spices. Simmer covered for 7 hours until the skin of the ham becomes lustrous on the surface. Remove the bag of spices. Place the ham, carefully, keeping it in shape, onto a large platter. Serve sliced either hot or cold. *Serves 10–12.*

CHERRY-COLORED FRIED PORK

T'ang Ts'u Ying T'ao Jou

In 1780, Emperor Ch'ien-lung made an inspection tour of southern China and stayed at the house of Chen Yüan Lung, where he enjoyed dishes prepared by Chen Tung Kuan whom he rewarded with silver. Chen Yuan Lung offered Chen Tung Kuan to the emperor, and it is noted in the records that this cook served his highness at the detached palace in Jehol, Manchuria. T'ang Ts'u Ying T'ao Jou was one of the dishes for which this cook was famous.

1 ¼ pounds fresh bacon with skin in ½" cubes
4 2" long pieces green onion plus ¼ cup green onion, chopped
½ tablespoon ginger root, sliced plus ½ tablespoon ginger root, chopped
½ teaspoon Five Spices (see page 35)
2 ¼ cups sesame oil plus 1 tablespoon sesame oil
4 tablespoons soy
2 tablespoons vinegar
2 tablespoons sugar

Put meat cubes in a pot with 2 times as much water as the volume of meat. Add onion, ginger slices and Five Spices, and bring to a boil over high heat. Lower heat to medium and cook covered 15 minutes. Remove cubes from the pot and drain well. Bring to a boil over high heat 2 ¼ cups sesame oil in a pan and put in the boiled pork and fry until light brown. In another pan, heat 1 tablespoon sesame oil and bring to a boil over high heat. Lower heat and add chopped onion and ginger, soy, vinegar, sugar, and fried pork. Stir briskly for two minutes or more and serve when the pork has turned cherry-colored. Serve hot. *Serves 3–4.*

DEEP-FRIED MEAT BALLS

Cha Wan Tzu

This Shantung dish was very popular in Peking. In the cooking of the populace, additional ingredients are used, such as potatoes, carrots, etc.

½ pound lean pork, chopped
½ pound fat pork, chopped
1 tablespoon green onion, chopped
½ tablespoon ginger root, chopped
2 eggs
1 tablespoon cornstarch
2 teaspoons salt
¼ teaspoon black pepper
2½ cups sesame oil
1 teaspoon peppercorns, parched and crushed (see page 37)

Mix well lean and fat pork, add onion, ginger, and eggs. Mix well and add cornstarch, 1 teaspoon salt, and black pepper, mixing thoroughly. Form meat balls of 1″ diameter. Bring sesame oil to a boil at high heat and put meat balls into the pan. Lower the heat and deep-fry for about 20 minutes or until the meat balls are browned. Serve hot. Crushed peppercorns and 1 teaspoon salt may be sprinkled on the meat balls, if desired. If the oil is too hot, only the surface of the balls are browned while the inside remains uncooked. However, if deep-fried too long, the balls become hard. *Serves 2–3.*

FILLET OF PORK WITH CORNSTARCH DRESSING

Ch'ao Liu Li Chi

This is a well-known Shantung dish.

¾ pound pork fillet, julienned
½ teaspoon black pepper
2½ tablespoons cornstarch
1¼ cups water
2½ cups sesame oil
2 tablespoons green onion, julienned
1 teaspoon ginger root, chopped
1 tablespoon soy
½ teaspoon salt
½ cup bamboo shoots (see page 33), julienned

Sprinkle pork strips with black pepper and mix well. Dissolve 1½ tablespoons cornstarch in ½ cup water and dip pork slices in the cornstarch dressing. Bring sesame oil to a boil over high heat and deep-fry pork strips until browned. In another pan, put 1 tablespoon of the sesame oil used in deep-frying and bring to a boil over high heat. Lower heat to medium and put in onion, ginger, soy, and salt and bring to a boil. Add ½ cup of water and bamboo shoots. Bring to a boil and add fried pork slices. Lastly, dissolve 1 tablespoon cornstarch in ¼ cup of water, pour over pork slices and bamboo shoots, stir well, and simmer uncovered until the liquid thickens. Serve hot. *Serves 2–3.*

FRIED AND STEAMED PORK WITH SKIN

Kou Jou

It was during the Ming Dynasty that this Chiangnan dish was introduced to the imperial court. It was often served at banquets.

2½ cups sesame oil
1 pound fresh bacon with skin
1 cup ½" long pieces green onion
⅔" cubed ginger root
½ pound vegetable greens, preserved with salt (see page 232), cut in 1" lengths
4 tablespoons soy
1 tablespoon wine
1 teaspoon sugar

Bring sesame oil to a boil, place the meat with skin side down in the pan, and deep-fry at high heat until the skin turns light brown. Remove from pan and cut into 1" cubes without removing the skin. Place cubed meat in another bowl with skin side down. Cover neatly with onion, ginger, and preserved vegetable greens. Add soy, wine, and sugar. Steam 2 hours and remove from the steamer. Cover with another larger bowl and invert so that the pork cubes are on the surface with the skin side up and vegetable greens are hidden underneath. Serve either hot or cold. This dish is rich and flavorous. *Serves 2–3.*

FRIED CHOPPED PORK

Ch'ao Jou Mo

This dish was devised by Empress Dowager Tzu-hsi. She also sandwiched this meat in a raised flour sesame cake known as *"sao bing,"* comparable to Parkerhouse rolls except for the sesame.

2 tablespoons sesame oil
½ pound lean pork, chopped
½ pound fat pork, chopped
1½ teaspoons ginger root, chopped
1 tablespoon green onion, chopped
½ cup green soy beans, fresh, boiled in water for 15 minutes, chopped (A half cup chopped peanuts, chopped walnuts, or pine seeds may be substituted.)
1 tablespoon soy
1 teaspoon salt

Bring sesame oil to a boil in a pan over high heat and fry chopped meat both lean and fat until almost dry. Add ginger and onion and stir well. Add soy beans, soy, and salt, and fry stirring constantly, until hardly any liquid remains. Serve hot. *Serves 2–3.*

FRIED MUTTON, SHEEP LIVER, AND KIDNEY

Pao San Yang

This Manchurian dish is loved by all Manchurians.

1 teaspoon garlic, chopped
1 tablespoon vinegar
1 tablespoon sesame oil
½ pound mutton, julienned
2 tablespoons green onion, chopped
2 teaspoons ginger root, chopped
6 tablespoons soy
½ pound sheep liver, julienned
½ pound sheep kidney, julienned

Combine chopped garlic with vinegar in a small dish. Bring sesame oil to a boil in a pan and fry mutton strips, onion, ginger, soy, liver, and kidney for a few seconds. Add garlic combined with vinegar. Stir briskly over high heat for a minute or so and serve piping hot. *Serves 2–3.*

FRIED PORK, EGGS, JUDAS' EARS, AND LICORICE FLOWERS

Ch'ao Mu Hsu Jou

5 eggs
1 teaspoon salt
⅓ teaspoon monosodium glutamate
½ cup and 3 tablespoons sesame oil
½ pound pork, julienned
¼ cup green onion, chopped
1 teaspoon ginger root, chopped
1½ tablespoons soy
1 tablespoon water
5 Judas' ears (see page 36)
7 dried licorice flowers (see page 36)

Beat eggs and season with salt and monosodium gluta-mate. Bring ½ cup of sesame oil to a boil in a pan and fry eggmixture. Tear into pieces with chopsticks and drain oil. In another pan bring 3 tablespoons sesame oil to boil. Fry pork, onion, and ginger and add soy and water. Mix well and cook until the pork is well done. Add Judas' ears, licorice flowers (both uncut), and fried eggmixture, and stir briskly for a few minutes. Serve hot. *Serves 2–3.*

MUTTON AND RADISH

Yang Jou Lo Pa

After the Manchurians had entered the main part of China, they adopted many Chinese customs but their fondness for mutton, which had been their staple food, remained unchanged. Peking acquired her supply of mutton from Mongolia, where Mongolian nomads grazed their sheep. Famous cooks in Peking took infinite care to devise new ways of preparing mutton to please the gourmets. Peking, therefore, became the center of the art of cooking mutton.

2 cups soy bean oil
1½ pounds radish, cut aslant in 1½″ × ½″ × ¼″ pieces
1½ pounds mutton, in ½″ cubes
1 cup 1½″ long pieces green onion
1″ cubed ginger root, crushed
1½ teaspoons peppercorns   *Placed in a cloth bag*
4 star aniseed
1 tablespoon wine
6 tablespoons soy
½ teaspoon salt or more to suit taste

Bring soy bean oil to a boil in an iron pan and fry radish until brown. In another pot, place mutton cubes with three times as much water and add onion and spices. Cook over low heat uncovered. Remove white scum when it rises to the surface. Keep boiling until the water is reduced to half its volume. Add wine, soy, salt, and radish when the mutton has become very tender and cook another ten minutes covered. Serve hot. Taste the radish before cooking, for a bitter radish is not savory. *Serves 5–6.*

PORK AND LOTUS LEAVES

He Yeh Jou

1 ½ *pounds pork flank in* ½ *" cubes*
½ *cup soy*
2 *tablespoons wine*
1 *teaspoon sugar*
½ *teaspoon salt*
½ *tablespoon ginger root, chopped*
2 *cups glutinous rice parched until browned, then ground and sifted*
3 *or 4 tender lotus leaves (see page 36), washed well and cut 5" squares*

Marinate the pork for 3 hours in a sauce of soy, wine, sugar, salt, and ginger. After draining, dredge pork well with ground rice powder. Wrap two or three pieces of pork in a lotus leaf and tie the small square package with a string. Steam packages for 1 hour. Serve hot on a plate still wrapped with lotus leaves. Each guest unwraps the package just before eating. *Serves 4–5.*

PORK KIDNEY AND BEAN CURD SKIN

Yao Ting Fu P'i

When this Shantung dish was introduced to the court is not known but it was often served at Empress Dowager Tzu-hsi's table.

1 cup pork stock (see page 42)
½ cup dried bean curd skin (see page 34) julienned
1 pork kidney about ⅓ pound (see page 37), cut ½″ cubes
1 tablespoon green onion, chopped
½″ cube ginger root, chopped
1 tablespoon soy
½ teaspoon salt
1 teaspoon cornstarch, dissolved in 1 tablespoon water
1 tablespoon wine

Heat the stock in a pot and bring to a boil over moderate heat. Put in bean curd skin and cook for five minutes uncovered. Add kidney, onion, ginger, soy, salt, and wine and bring to a boil. Add cornstarch paste and simmer a few seconds. Serve hot. This dish must not be served cold or reheated. *Serves 1–2.*

PORK SLICES FRIED AND SIMMERED IN CORNSTARCH DRESSING

Liu Jou P'ien

A popular northern Chinese dish, mentioned in a publication known as *Tung Ching Men Hua Lu* published during the Sung Dynasty, was introduced to the imperial court during the Ming Dynasty.

¾ pound fresh pork tenderloin cut in 1″ × ½″ × ⅛″ slices
2 tablespoons cornstarch
1 tablespoon green onion, chopped
½″ cube ginger root, chopped
3 tablespoons soy
1 teaspoon sugar
1 tablespoon wine
2 egg whites
½ cup water
4 tablespoons sesame oil

Dust pork slices with 1 tablespoon cornstarch. Combine in a bowl onion, ginger, soy, sugar, wine, 1 tablespoon cornstarch, egg whites, and water and mix well. Bring sesame oil to a boil. Remove from fire, put in pork, and fry for 3 minutes over high heat. Lower heat to medium. Add combined ingredients and simmer, stirring constantly, until the liquid thickens. Serve hot. *Serves 2.*

SOOCHOW STYLE DISH

Su Tsa Chou Tzu

This dish was introduced to the imperial court by the famous cook, Chen Tung Kuan, from Soochow Province. Meals in northern China were originally thin in taste and greasy, but Chen Tung Kuan improved them and devised dishes with variety in taste and without greasiness of which this is one of the most typical. *Su* means Soochow Province, *tsa* means kitchen. Therefore, this is called the Soochow Style Dish.

2½ cups sesame oil
2½ pounds fresh ham with skin
1 carrot 1″ × 5″
2 pieces ginger root in ¼″ cubes
1 piece dried orange peel about 1″ square
½ teaspoon licorice root, chopped
½ cup soy
1 teaspoon crystal sugar (1 teaspoon granulated sugar may be substituted.)
2 dried mushrooms (see page 36), julienned
2 tablespoons wine
4 1″ long pieces green onion
1¼ cups water

Bring sesame oil to a boil in a pan and fry the ham until it becomes light brown. In another pot, put ham, carrot, 1 piece ginger, dried orange peel, licorice root, and fill the pot with enough water to cover the ham. Cook for 1 hour over moderate heat covered. Then transfer the ham only into a smaller pot, preferably an earthen pot. Add soy, sugar, mushrooms, wine, onion, 1 piece ginger

(Continued at bottom of next page)

STEAMED PORK

Pai Jou

It was a custom in Manchuria to sacrifice a hog on the Festival of Ancestors held twice a year and on these occasions, the emperor participated by eating some portion of the sacrificed hog. *Pai Jou* originated from this Manchurian custom.

1 pound fresh bacon
2 2" long pieces green onion and 1 teaspoon green onion, chopped
½" cube ginger root, crushed, and 1 teaspoon ginger root, chopped
1 teaspoon garlic, chopped
4 tablespoons soy

Place meat in a medium-sized pot half filled with water, add ginger cube and 2 pieces of onion and boil for 20 minutes covered. Remove the pork from the pot, cut in slices of 2½" × ½", arrange on a dish and steam for 1 hour. Serve the pork with a sauce of chopped onion, ginger, garlic, and soy, well mixed to taste. Serve hot. *Serves 2.*

(Continued from previous page)
and 1¼ cups of water. Simmer uncovered for 1½ hours over moderate heat, basting frequently, until hardly any liquid remains. Slice and serve hot or cold. To brown the meat with oil is to seal its flavor. Licorice root and dried orange peel are used to refine the flavor of the pork. *Serves 4–5.*

SPICED MUTTON SPREAD

Shao Yang Jou

Emperor Hsüan Tung was very fond of this Manchurian dish.

2 pounds mutton in ¼" cubes
5 cups water
10 tablespoons soy
2 cups 2" long pieces green onion
2 pieces ginger root in ½" cubes

½ teaspoon Five Spices (see page 35)
1 dried orange peel about 1" square
1 ¾" long piece licorice root — *Placed in a cloth bag*
3 pieces cardamom

3 to 4 cups sesame oil

Put mutton cubes and water in a pot and simmer over low heat. Add soy, onion, spices, and ginger. Cook covered until the mutton becomes so tender as to almost break, about two hours. Add water if the soup runs dry. Remove the mutton and spices from the pot, but save the broth. In another pan bring sesame oil to a boil over high heat and deep-fry cooked mutton for five minutes. Remove from the pan, drain, and mash in a bowl. Place the mutton back into its original pot of soup and cook uncovered until hardly any liquid remains. This dish will keep for about a week in a cool place. Serve hot or cold. It is wonderful served as a spread on crackers with cocktails. *Serves 4–5.*

STEAMED PORK, KELP, AND GREEN ONIONS

Su Jou

This dish originated in Honan Province. It is delicious served with wine.

1¾ pounds pork loin, in ¼" slices
2½ cups 2½" long pieces green onion
1 sheet of kelp 18" × 4", washed and cut in 2¼" lengths
2 tablespoons ginger root, julienned
1 teaspoon sugar
2½ tablespoons soy
1 tablespoon wine
2 tablespoons vinegar
1 tablespoon sesame oil
1 teaspoon salt or more to suit taste
½ cup water

In a steamer place a bowl containing two layers of pork, onion, and kelp, interspersed with slivers of ginger. Combine sugar, soy, wine, vinegar, sesame oil, salt, and water, and mix well. Pour over the pork, kelp, and onion, taking care that the layers are well covered by the sauce. Seal the cover of the steamer with paper and steam for 1½ hours. Serve hot. When arranging on a dish, place onion and kelp separately from the pork. *Serves 3–4.*

VEGETABLES

BRAISED BAMBOO SHOOTS WITH SOY

Hung Shao Yü Lan P'ien

This Chiangnan dish was introduced to the imperial court during the reign of Emperor Ch'ien-lung.

1 ¼ cups sesame oil
½ pound dried bamboo shoots (*see page 33*)
1 tablespoon lard
1 teaspoon green onion, chopped
½ teaspoon ginger root, chopped
1 teaspoon dried shrimp (*see page 38*)
1 tablespoon soy
1 tablespoon wine
1 teaspoon sugar
3 tablespoons water

Bring sesame oil to a boil in a pan and fry bamboo shoots for 2 minutes over high temperature. Take care to cover the pan immediately for the oil will splatter violently. Drain. Melt lard in another pan, put in onion and ginger, and stir. Add shrimp, soy, wine, sugar, and water. Bring to a boil and add bamboo. Cook uncovered until hardly any liquid remains. Serve hot. *Serves 2–3.*

CHESTNUTS AND CHINESE CABBAGE

Li Tzu Pai Ts'ai

1 cup peanut oil
1 pound Chinese cabbage, leaves separated and washed
2 tablespoons lard
1½ cups chestnuts, boiled, shelled, skinned, and quartered
⅓ cup dried shrimp (see page 38)
1 teaspoon ginger root, julienned
½ cup soy
2 tablespoons sugar
2 cups chicken stock (see page 41)
8 medium-sized dried mushrooms (see page 36), julienned
½ teaspoon monosodium glutamate

Bring peanut oil to a boil over high heat. Fry Chinese cabbage leaves one by one until tender, and drain. Heat lard in another pan over high heat and add ginger, shrimp, and chestnuts and fry 1 minute. Add soy, sugar, and stock, stir well, and bring to a boil. Add mushrooms, fried cabbage, and monosodium glutamate and mix well. Lower heat to medium and simmer covered for 35 minutes. Serve hot. This dish is rich in flavor and most delightful. *Serves 4–5.*

EGGPLANT SALAD

Leng Pan Ch'ieh Tzu

1 ½ pounds eggplant, washed
1 cup dried shrimp (see page 38)
2 tablespoons seasame oil
3 tablespoons sesame paste
3 tablespoons green onion, chopped
1 teaspoon ginger root, chopped
1 teaspoon garlic, chopped
3 ½ tablespoons soy
1 teaspoon vinegar
½ teaspoon sugar
1 teaspoon peppercorn oil (see page 37)

Boil eggplant over slow fire, turning over frequently until tender inside. Cool and peel with fingers. Put in a bowl and mash. Place mashed eggplant on one half of a large dish. Bring sesame oil to a boil and fry shrimp. Chop fine and place them on one quarter of the dish and sesame paste on to the other quarter of the dish. Combine the rest of the ingredients for a sauce. Serve cold eggplant, shrimp, and sesame paste on a dish with a bowl of the above sauce. Just before serving, marinate eggplant and shrimp with the sauce. Serve cold. *Serves 4–5.*

FRIED AND COOKED CARROTS, PORK, SOY BEANS, AND BEAN CURD

Ch'ao Hu Lo Pa Chiang

2 cups sesame oil
1½ pounds bean curd cut in ½" cubes
1 pound pork in ½" cubes
1 tablespoon ginger root, chopped
½ cup green onion, chopped
½ cup soy
2 carrots, about 1" × 5", pared and cut in ½" cubes
2 cups pork stock (see page 42)
½ cup fresh green soy beans, skinned, cut lengthwise in halves, and boiled 15 minutes
½ teaspoon monosodium glutamate

Bring to a boil 1¾ cups sesame oil in a pan over high heat, fry bean curd cubes until brown, and drain. In another pan bring to a boil ¼ cup of sesame oil over high heat, and put in ginger, onion, soy, and pork. Fry uncovered for 3 minutes, then add carrots and stock. Bring to a boil and cook until the carrots are tender and the pork is well done. Add soy beans, fried bean curd cubes, and monosodium glutamate. Bring to a boil and lower heat to medium. Simmer, stirring frequently, uncovered for 3 minutes or more. Serve hot. *Serves 6–7.*

FRIED AND COOKED EGGPLANT

Shao Ch'ieh Tzu

1 cup and 1 tablespoon sesame oil

5 eggplant or ¾ pounds (*Oriental eggplant is small in size*),
   washed, sliced in ¼″ thickness, scored 1/8″ deep on one side

1½ tablespoons green onion, julienned

1 teaspoon ginger root, chopped

½ cup pork, julienned

1 tablespoon soy

1 teaspoon salt

½ teaspoon monosodium glutamate

1 tablespoon dried shrimp (*see page 38*)

1 cup bamboo shoots (*see page 33*), cut in 2″ × 1½″ × ¼″
   pieces

½ cup dried mushrooms (*see page 36*), julienned

¼ teaspoon garlic, chopped

1 cup water

2 teaspoons cornstarch dissolved in 3 tablespoons water

Bring 1 cup of sesame oil to a boil in a pan and fry eggplant slices until tender and nearly scorched. Remove
from the pan and drain well. Heat 1 tablespoon oil in
another pan, put in onion, ginger, and pork, and fry,
stirring briskly, until the pork is well done. Add soy,
salt, monosodium glutamate, and shrimp, bring to a boil,
and add bamboo shoots and mushrooms. Stir well and
fry 1 minute. Add garlic and water. Then add the fried
eggplant slices and bring to a boil. Simmer covered for
3 minutes and add cornstarch paste. Stir well and cook
until the liquid thickens. Serve hot. *Serves 4–5.*

FRIED TURNIPS

Kuo Shao Lo Pa

6 tablespoons sesame oil
2 cups turnip, pared, cut aslant in 1" × ½" pieces
¼ cup green onion, chopped
½ teaspoon ginger root, chopped
½ pound pork, chopped
4 tablespoons soy
2 tablespoons water
½ teaspoon monosodium glutamate
1 teaspoon cornstarch dissolved in 3 tablespoons water

Bring 3 tablespoons sesame oil to a boil in a pan, and fry turnips until brown. Heat 3 tablespoons sesame oil over high heat in another pan, add onion, ginger, pork, soy, and water, and mix well. After boil is reached, lower heat and simmer covered for 4 minutes. Add fried turnip and monosodium glutamate. Then add cornstarch paste and stir well. Simmer over moderate heat, stirring constantly, until thickened. Serve hot. *Serves 2–3.*

STEAMED CHINESE CABBAGE AND HAM

Huo Tui Cheng Pai Ts'ai

During the Chinese Imperial Regime, the highest quality Chinese cabbage was grown in Shantung and the finest ham was produced in Chinhua, Chiangnan. Due to poor and slow transportation, they were hard to procure in Northern China, and, therefore, in those days this dish was considered a delicacy, esteemed for its rarity.

1 tablespoon lard

¾ pound Chinese cabbage, inside part only, cut in 1" × 2" pieces

¼ cup green onion, cut slantwise in 1" pieces

2 teaspoons ginger root, sliced

1 tablespoon dried shrimp (see page 38)

½ pound Chinese ham or bacon cut in 1¼" × ½" × ⅛" slices

1 cup pork stock (see page 42)

1 teaspoon salt or more if necessary

½ teaspoon monosodium glutamate

Melt the lard in a pan and fry Chinese cabbage pieces. Arrange attractively half of the following ingredients in a bowl: cabbage, onion, ginger, shrimps, and Chinese ham. Then place the other half over the first layer. Add pork stock, salt, and monosodium glutamate. Place the bowl in a steamer and steam 40 minutes over high heat. Serve hot. *Serves 2–3.*

STEWED STRING BEANS

Men Pien Tou

This was a popular Peking dish.

2 tablespoons sesame oil
½ pound fresh bacon, julienned in 1" slivers
1½ tablespoons green onion, julienned
1 teaspoon ginger root, julienned
1 tablespoon soy
1 teaspoon salt
1 cup water
¾ pound string beans, washed, ends removed, strung, and cut
   in 1" lengths

Bring sesame oil to a boil and add meat, onion, and ginger. Fry while stirring. Add soy and bring to a boil. Add water and bring to a boil. Add string beans, mix well, and cover. Simmer over low heat for 30 minutes or until hardly any liquid remains. Serve hot. *Serves 2–3.*

STUFFED MARROW

Tung Kua Chung

1 marrow (see page 36), about 6" diameter, washed and peeled. Cut off upper quarter to make a lid, remove seeds, and wash inside.

½ *cup green onion in* ½" *cubes*

1 teaspoon ginger root, chopped

½ *cup bamboo shoots in* ¼" *cubes*

½ *cup dried mushrooms in* ¼" *cubes (see page 36)*

1 cup crab meat, fresh or canned

1 teaspoon sesame oil

1 tablespoon wine

¾ *teaspoon salt or more to suit taste*

½ *teaspoon monosodium glutamate*

Stuff the marrow with all ingredients after they have been mixed well together. Cover with lid and steam for 1 hour. Serve hot. In China it was customary to leave a section of the peel and inscribe on it "The world is one family" or something similar. *Serves 3–4.*

SWEET AND SOUR CUCUMBERS

T'ang Ts'u Huang Kua

3 tablespoons sesame oil
10 peppercorns
3 tablespoons soy
1 tablespoon sugar
3 tablespoons vinegar
½ cup green onion, julienned
1 cup cucumbers, (unpared, if skin is tender), cut in 1¼" ×
   ½" × ½" pieces

Bring the sesame oil to a boil in a pan, add peppercorns,
and fry. Add soy, sugar, vinegar, and onion. Stir well
and simmer. Add cucumbers. Fry uncovered over high
heat until the liquid turns into syrup and yet the cucumbers remain fresh in color. Serve hot. *Serves 2–3.*

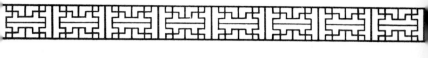

BUDDHIST DISHES

BAMBOO SHOOTS AND MUSHROOMS
FRIED AND SIMMERED WITH SOY

Shao Erh Tung

6 tablespoons soy bean oil
½ pound bamboo shoots (see page 33), julienned
1½ teaspoons ginger root, chopped
1 teaspoon garlic, chopped
¼ pound Mongolian mushrooms (dried mushrooms may be sub-
    stituted, see page 36), julienned
3 tablespoons soy
½ teaspoon sugar
½ cup water

Bring 5 tablespoons oil to a boil in a pan and fry bamboo shoots for a minute or two over high heat, stirring briskly. Remove from the pan. Bring to a boil 1 tablespoon oil in another pan and fry ginger, garlic, bamboo shoots, and mushrooms for 1 minute, then add soy, sugar, and water. Stir well and bring to a boil. Lower heat to moderate and simmer uncovered for 30 minutes until hardly any liquid remains. Serve hot or cold. *Serves 2.*

BRAISED STEAMED DOUGH
WITH SOY AND BAMBOO

Hung Shao Mien Chin

This temple dish was prepared on New Year's Day in the imperial court.

1 cup flour
¼ cup water
1 tablespoon sesame oil
1 tablespoon ginger root, chopped
2 tablespoons soy
½ teaspoon sugar
¼ pound bamboo shoots (see page 33), julienned
½ cup water

Mix flour and ¼ cup of water, knead into a hard dough, and let stand 15 minutes. Rinse the dough in a bowl of water and wash off the soft flossy surface until only the hard core remains. Roll remaining core into a bar, place in a steamer, and steam for 20 minutes. Cut steamed dough into ⅓″ cubes. Heat sesame oil in a pan and bring to a boil over high heat, put in ginger and steamed dough and fry a few minutes. Add soy, sugar, ½ cup of water, and bamboo shoots. Lower heat and simmer uncovered for 20 minutes until there remains hardly any liquid. Serve hot or cold. *Serves 3–4.*

FRIED BAMBOO SHOOTS, MUSHROOMS, AND CUCUMBERS

Ch'ao San Hsien

2 tablespoons sesame oil
1 teaspoon ginger root, minced
¼ cup bamboo shoots (see page 33), julienned
¼ cup medium-sized dried mushrooms (see page 36), julienned
3 tablespoons soy
½ teaspoon sugar
¼ cup cucumbers, julienned

Heat sesame oil in a pan over high heat and bring to a boil. Put in ginger and fry for 1 minute. Add bamboo shoots and fry for 2 minutes. Add mushrooms, stir, and add soy and sugar. Fry, stirring constantly, for 2 minutes. Lastly, add cucumber and fry, stirring constantly, over high heat for 1 minute. Place in a bowl and serve hot. Cook quickly. Be careful when frying cucumbers, for they lose freshness if overfried while the taste is flat if undercooked. *Serves 1–2.*

FRIED BEAN CURD SKIN
WITH CORNSTARCH DRESSING

Liu Fu P'i

This is a Buddhist temple dish which has another name, Su Yü Tu, meaning a vegetable dish in the shape of a fish's stomach.

1¾ cups sesame oil
¼ pound dried bean curd skin (see page 33), cut in 1" × ½" slices
1 tablespoon green onion, chopped
1 teaspoon ginger root, chopped
2 tablespoons soy
½ teaspoon salt
1 tablespoon sugar
1 tablespoon wine
¾ cup bean sprout stock (see page 44)
1 cup bamboo shoots (see page 33), julienned
8 medium-sized dried mushrooms (see page 36), julienned
1 tablespoon cornstarch dissolved in 3 tablespoons water

Bring 1½ cups sesame oil to a boil over high heat, lower the heat to medium and fry bean curd skin without scorching until slightly brown. Bring to a boil over high heat ¼ cup sesame oil in another pan, add onion, ginger, soy, salt, sugar, wine, and bean sprout stock, and again bring to a boil. Reduce heat to low, add fried bean curd skin, bamboo shoots, and mushrooms, and cook covered until the bean curd becomes tender. Add cornstarch paste, stirring constantly, until the liquid thickens. Serve hot. *Serves 2–3.*

MASHED MOUNTAIN POTATOES

Shan Yao Ni

During an inspection tour of South China, Emperor Ch'ien-lung, who was fond of sweet foods, enjoyed the following dish offered by Yen Hao clan. Upon his return to the imperial court, he ordered it to be entered in the list of imperial recipes.

1 pound mountain potatoes (see page 36), pared, and cut in irregular pieces
2 tablespoons sugar
2 tablespoons lard, rendered

Put mountain potatoes in a pot of water and cook covered over moderate heat for 30 minutes until the potatoes become tender. Drain. Mash the potatoes in a bowl, add sugar, mix well, and whip. Melt the lard in a pan, add the mashed potatoes and mix well. Place the pan over fire, heat steadily, stirring constantly, over moderate heat for 4 to 5 minutes. Serve hot. This dish must appear fluffy and pretty. You must eat it slowly because it might choke you. *Serves 2.*

SALTED BEANS
FRIED WITH SOY BEAN CURD CAKES

Tou Ch'ih Ch'ao Tou Fu

This vegetarian dish was originated by Buddhists and it was prepared in most Chinese families on the Buddhist abstinence day. It is not known when it was introduced to the court, but the imperial household kitchen used to prepare it at the beginning of the New Year. Sometimes the emperor gave this dish to a minister as a meritorious award. Tsu Yen Chai Diary, written on January 10, 1920, by Chi-ling, the last household minister of Ch'ing Dynasty, states: "The Emperor presented me a dish of Tou Ch'ih Ch'ao Tou Fu and a dish of Su Shao Lo Pa for lunch."

1½ cups sesame oil
1½ pounds bean curd cut in ½" cubes
1 teaspoon sesame oil
2 tablespoons salted beans (see page 34)
5 pieces ginger in ½" cubes
2½ teaspoons soy
½ cup water
1 tablespoon sugar
1 teaspoon salt

Bring 1½ cups sesame oil to a boil in a pan, put in bean curd cubes, and fry over moderate heat until yellowish. In another pan, parch black salted beans in 1 teaspoon sesame oil, add other ingredients, and bring to a boil. Put in fried bean curd, simmer 10 minutes or more covered over medium heat until hardly any liquid remains. Serve hot. *Serves 3.*

SPINACH WITH SAUCE

Pan Po Ts'ai

A northern Chinese dish that is delicious in summer. Princess Tsung used to prepare this recipe for Emperor Hsüan T'ung who enjoyed it very much. It was entered in the list of imperial recipes. In 1940 Princess Tsung, a relative of the former Emperor, personally taught Princess Aichingioro to prepare this dish.

1 pound spinach, washed thoroughly
½ cup dried shrimp (see page 38)
3 tablespoons sesame oil
2 tablespoons soy
½ teaspoon salt
1 teaspoon sugar
1 teaspoon vinegar
1 teaspoon mustard dissolved in 1 tablespoon water
1 tablespoon sesame paste (see page 38)
2 tablespoons green onion, chopped
¼ teaspoon ginger root, chopped
1 teaspoon peppercorn oil (see page 37)

Put spinach in a pot half-filled with boiling water and cook until tender. Do not cover the pot lest the spinach turn yellow. Bring sesame oil to a boil in a pan, fry shrimp, remove from the pan, and chop fine. After draining, chop the spinach until pulpy, then wrap in a cloth and press to remove water. Place spinach in a bowl. Prepare a sauce with soy, salt, sugar, vinegar, mustard paste, sesame paste, onion, ginger, and peppercorn oil. Just before serving, mix the spinach with chopped shrimp and marinate with the sauce. Serve cold. *Serves 3–4.*

STEAMED BROCADE-LIKE ARRAY OF VEGETABLES WITH BEAN CURD

Ch'ing Cheng Shih Chin Tou Fu

Empress dowagers of the Ch'ing Dynasty were fond of tender food because of their bad teeth. The following Buddhist temple dish was one of their favorites.

2 medium-sized dried mushrooms (see page 36), julienned

½ cup bamboo shoots (see page 33), julienned

¼ cup Judas' ears (see page 36)

10 small white chrysanthemums, petals only; if dried use whole flowers (see page 35)

20 lotus seeds (see page 36)

20 gingko nuts (see page 35)

½ cup lotus root, pared and julienned

¼ cup vegetable greens, pickled (see page 232), cut in ½" pieces

2 tablespoons ginger root, chopped

¾ pound bean curd cut in ¼" × ½" × 1" pieces

1 pound bean sprouts, boiled 30 minutes in 4 cups water; only stock is used

1 tablespoon sesame oil

2½ teaspoons salt or more to suit taste

¼ cup cucumbers, pared and julienned

Place neatly at the bottom of a large bowl mushrooms, bamboo shoots, Judas' ears, chrysanthemums, lotus seeds, gingko nuts, lotus root, vegetable greens, and ginger root. Place pieces of bean curd over them and pour in bean sprout stock, filling the bowl half full. Add sesame oil and salt. Place bowl in a steamer and steam at high heat for 30 minutes. After removing bowl from steamer, sprinkle slivers of cucumber on top as garnish. Serve hot. *Serves 4–5.*

VEGETABLES FRIED AND SIMMERED

Lo Han Chai

Temples in China were so wealthy that the priests were able to be extremely particular about food, and dishes prepared in such a temple as the Kun Tsin Temple in Peking gained a nationwide reputation. From the first through the fifth of January, it was the custom of the Manchurians to eat vegetarian food which followed closely the Buddhist temple recipes, such as the following:

2½ cups sesame oil
½ cup yams, julienned
½ cup carrots, julienned
½ cup bean curd in ½" cubes
1 tablespoon soy
1½ tablespoons ginger root, chopped
½ pound Chinese cabbage in 1" cubes
2 cups water
½ cup Judas' ears (see page 36)
½ cup dried bean curd skin (see page 34) cut in 1" × ¼" pieces
½ cup dried mushrooms (see page 36) cut in 1" × ¼" pieces
¼ cup chrysanthemum flowers (see page 35)
¼ cup small dried day lilies (see page 35)
2 teaspoons salt

Bring the sesame oil to a boil in a pan, add yams, carrots, and bean curd, fry for 3 minutes, and drain. Put soy in another pan and bring to a boil over high heat. Add chopped ginger, Chinese cabbage, and water. Stir and bring to a boil. Add Judas' ears, bean curd skin, mushrooms, chrysanthemums, day lilies, yam, carrot, bean curd, and salt. Lower heat and simmer uncovered for 40 minutes. Serve hot. Although this dish is not attractive in appearance, its flavor is delicious. *Serves 4–5.*

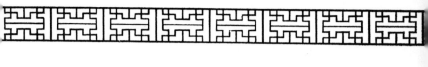

FLOWERS

CLEAR CHICKEN SOUP WITH JASMINE

Ch'ing T'ang Mo Li

This is a noted Chiangnan Province dish. The floating jasmine petals lend their delicate fragrance to the chicken soup.

5 pounds poulard, dressed
5 cups clear chicken stock (see page 41)
2 teaspoons salt
½ teaspoon monosodium glutamate
1 teaspoon green onion, julienned
1 teaspoon ginger root, julienned
¼ cup bamboo shoots (see page 33), julienned
¼ cup dried mushrooms (see page 36), julienned
½ cup fresh jasmine petals (see page 36)

Place chicken in a pot, pour in enough water to cover and bring to a boil over high heat. Lower heat and simmer uncovered until water volume is reduced by half. Remove chicken, cut off breasts, and julienne into 1″ slivers. Bring clear chicken stock to a boil over high heat. Add salt, monosodium glutamate, onion, ginger root, slivers of chicken, bamboo shoots, and mushrooms. Cook uncovered for 10 minutes over medium heat. Remove the contents from the pot into a large bowl. Sprinkle with jasmine petals and serve hot immediately. *Serves 5–6.*

CHRYSANTHEMUMS AND JULIENNED CHICKEN MEAT

Chü Hua Chi Szu

2 tablespoons sesame oil

¾ pound chicken meat, skin removed, julienned

1 ½ tablespoons cornstarch, ½ tablespoon dissolved in 2 tablespoons water

1 teaspoon salt

1 teaspoon green onion, chopped

1 teaspoon ginger root, chopped

1 ½ teaspoons sugar dissolved in 1 cup water

30 small white chrysanthemums, petals only, if dried, use whole
flowers (see page 35)

Bring sesame oil to a boil and remove pan from fire. Add chicken meat dusted with cornstarch and sprinkled with salt. Stir briskly and fry with the heat of the pan. Add onion and ginger, and replace pan over fire and fry 2 minutes. Add cornstarch and sugar dissolved in water. When the liquid thickens, add chrysanthemum petals, stir and simmer for 2 seconds. Serve hot. Chrysanthemums cooked more than 2 seconds will turn bitter. *Serves 2.*

DAY LILIES COOKED WITH JULIENNED PORK

Huang Hua Shao Jou Szu

The following dish is enjoyed on Chung Yang Festival, held on the 9th of September. Day lilies are said to have protective powers.

3 tablespoons sesame oil
½ pound pork, julienned
½ tablespoon cornstarch
1 ½ tablespoons green onion, julienned
½ teaspoon ginger root, julienned
1 tablespoon soy
½ teaspoon salt or more if necessary
½ teaspoon sugar
½ tablespoon wine
¼ pound dried day lilies (see page 35)

Bring the sesame oil to a boil over high heat in a pan and add pork dusted with cornstarch, onion and ginger. Fry, stirring constantly, for 3 minutes over high heat. Season with soy, salt, sugar, and wine. Fry for 1 or 2 minutes, then add day lilies and fry, stirring constantly, for 2 minutes or more until the lilies have absorbed the flavor of the pork. Serve hot. *Serves 2.*

FRIED TUBEROSES

Cha Yü Chung Pan

1 cup peanut oil
20 tuberoses (see page 38)
1 egg white
2 tablespoons starch   } *mixed into a batter*
1½ teaspoons sugar
1 tablespoon water

Bring the oil to a boil in a pan over high heat to overcome its peculiar odor, and then lower the heat to medium. Dip tuberoses in a batter of egg white, starch, sugar, and water. Deep-fry flowers until slightly yellowish. Serve hot. Be careful when frying flowers not to overheat the oil, for the flowers will become scorched and taste bitter. *Serves 2–3.*

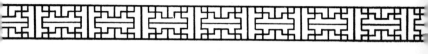

FRUITS
AND
NUTS

ALMOND CURD

Hsing Jen Tou Fu

Here is the traditional recipe and a modern method of preparing the Almond Curd. The combination of almond juice, arrowroot starch, and sugar is used as a cough medicine in China.

2¼ *teaspoons agar-agar (or 1 package gelatine)*
2½ *tablespoons sugar*
1½ *cups water*
20 *shelled almonds (blanched, chopped fine, crushed, and mixed well with ½ cup water. The juice is squeezed through a cloth and the dregs are discarded.) The modern method is to use 4 tablespoons prepared almond powder mixed in ½ cup of water.*
2 *drops of almond extract (Although the ancient recipe does not mention almond extract, the flavor of the curd is improved if 2 drops are added to the almond liquid when prepared from whole almonds.)*
1 *cup hot water*

Heat and dissolve agar-agar in 1½ cups water, add 1½ tablespoons sugar and almond juice. Bring to a boil once (add almond extract, if desired) and pour in a flat bowl 2½″ deep. Remove any scum on the surface. Allow it to stand until firm. Make criss-cross scores of 1″ × 2″ into the curd and insert a knife around the inner rim of the bowl to detach the curd. Pour 1 tablespoon sugar dissolved in 1 cup of hot water over the curd. For a modern touch serve with fruit juice or fresh or canned fruit cocktail. Serve cold. This dessert is wonderful after a multiple-course Chinese dinner. *Serves* 4.

FRIED BANANAS

Cha Hsiang Chiao

In the olden days when bananas were scarce in Peking, this dish was highly appreciated as a rare dessert.

2½ cups sesame oil
5 bananas 8" long, peeled, strings removed, and cut in 1" pieces
2 egg whites
1 tablespoon sugar   } *mixed into a batter*
4 tablespoons cornstarch
½ cup water

Bring the sesame oil to a boil in a pan over high heat and fry the banana pieces, previously dipped in a well mixed batter of egg whites, sugar, starch, and water. Fry until the banana pieces turn yellowish. Serve hot. *Serves 5–6.*

LOTUS ROOT STUFFED WITH GLUTINOUS RICE

Lo Mi Ou

Lo Mi Ou is one of the many kinds of summer refreshment which used to be enjoyed in the ancient city of Peking.

1 pound lotus root, washed, and both ends removed
⅓ cup glutinous rice; let stand 24 hours in 1 cup water, and drain
4 tablespoons sugar
1 teaspoon rose essence (see page 37)
4 tablespoons hot water
½ cup lotus seeds (see page 36)

With a chopstick stuff the lotus root holes with rice mixed with 2 tablespoons sugar. Steam the lotus root for 1½ hours and cool. Cut it into ½″ rings. Boil lotus seeds for 35 minutes in a pot with 2 cups water over moderate temperature. Serve cold lotus seeds on a dish with the lotus rings, and a bowl of rose essence combined with 2 tablespoons sugar and 4 tablespoons hot water for dipping lotus rings. Serve cold. Take care to fill all of the holes of the lotus root. Serve cold. *Serves 4–5.*

PEACH SOUP

T'ao Keng

3 tablespoons sugar
2 tablespoons cornstarch
1 cup water
1 tablespoon lard
½ pound peaches, pared, seeded, and mashed
1 teaspoon rose essence (see page 37)

Combine in a bowl sugar, cornstarch and water. Bring lard to a boil in a pan. Remove the pan from fire, add the contents of bowl, and mix well. Replace the pan over fire, add mashed peaches, stirring constantly, and cook until the contents come to a boil. Add rose essence. Serve either hot or cold. *Serves 2–3.*

STEAMED LOTUS SEEDS WITH HAWS JELLY CAKE

Ch'ing Cheng Lien Tzu

Since lotus seeds are very rich in vitamins, they are considered precious and are enjoyed by elderly people.

6 cups water
1 pound haws (see page 36)
2 cups and 5 tablespoons sugar
4 tablespoons cornstarch
3/4 pound lotus seeds (see page 36)
1 teaspoon lard

Boil haws in an uncovered pot with 2 cups water until tender. Purée and cook with 2 cups sugar and 4 tablespoons cornstarch until thickened. Pour in a square container and cool until the jelly hardens. Slice in 1/8″ × ½″ × ½″ pieces. Boil lotus seeds in a pot with 2 cups water or more for 45 minutes covered. In another pot bring to a boil 2 cups of water and 5 tablespoons sugar. Pour in a bowl, add lard and lotus seeds, and steam for 20 minutes. Serve hot with cold haws jelly cake. *Serves 4–5.*

COLD DISHES

ARC SHELLFISH AND CELERY

Ch'ing Ch'ih Ke

20 arc shellfish (see page 33)
3 8" celery stalks, strung, washed with salt water, cut in 1½"
   pieces
5 tablespoons soy
2 tablespoons vinegar
½ teaspoon sugar
½ teaspoon salt
1 tablespoon green onion, chopped
½ tablespoon ginger root, chopped
½ tablespoon ginger root, chopped
¾ teaspoon sesame oil
1 tablespoon wine

After the shellfish and the celery have been washed, place shellfish flat in a collander and parboil. Arrange them neatly on half of a platter. Parboil celery and place it on the other half of the platter. Marinate the shellfish and celery with a sauce of soy, vinegar, sugar, salt, onion, ginger, sesame oil, and wine just before serving. Serve chilled. *Serves 3–4.*

CHICKEN AND CUCUMBER WITH SAUCE

Chi Szu Pan Huang Kua

This dish was originally from Shantung.

2 pounds poulard, dressed

1 1" long piece green onion and 1 teaspoon green onion chopped

3 pieces ginger root in ½" cubes and 1 teaspoon ginger root, chopped

3 cups water

2 cucumbers 6" × 1", julienned (pared if skin is tough)

2 tablespoons soy

1 tablespoon sesame paste

1 teaspoon peppercorn oil (see page 37)

½ teaspoon mustard

3 tablespoons water

1 teaspoon salt

Place the chicken in a pot with 1" piece onion, 3 ginger cubes, and water, and bring to a boil at high heat. Reduce heat to low and simmer covered for 1 hour. Tear off the chicken meat and julienne into 1" slivers. Combine in a small bowl, soy, sesame paste, peppercorn oil, mustard, chopped green onion, chopped ginger, 3 tablespoons water, and salt. Mix well into a rich sauce. Arrange chicken strips on one half of a dish and cucumber strips on the other half and serve with a bowl of the sauce. Just before serving, marinate the chicken and cucumber with the sauce. Serve chilled. *Serves 3–4.*

CH'ING STYLE PRESERVED MEAT

Ch'ing Chiang Jou

The ham produced in Chinhua, Chiangnan, was very famous, but it was so salty that Emperor Ch'ien-lung directed his cook Chen Tung Kuan, to devise a new recipe. As a result, the following recipe was produced and became a specialty of Peking.

4½ pounds fresh bacon
2 quarts soy
1 tablespoon sugar
5 small pieces fennel
1 teaspoon Five Spices
2 teaspoons licorice root, chopped

Wash pork well, dry with a cloth, and put in a large earthen pot. Add a mixture of soy, sugar, fennel, Five Spices, and licorice root. Cover and seal the pot and place it in a dark cool place for four days. Remove the pork and place on a dish. Steam in a steamer for 1 hour over high heat. Remove and cool. Cut in 1″ × 2″ × ¼″ slices. Serve cold. *Serves 8–9.*

CRAB MEAT EGG ROLL

Hsieh Fen Tan Chuan

1 pound crab meat, fresh or canned, bones removed
1 ⅓ tablespoons cornstarch
4 eggs
1 teaspoon sugar
1 tablespoon green onion, chopped
½ tablespoon ginger root, chopped
1 teaspoon salt
⅓ teaspoon monosodium glutamate
¼ cup carrots, grated

Combine 1 tablespoon cornstarch, 1 egg white, sugar onion, ginger, and ½ teaspoon salt with crab meat and mix well. Break 2 eggs, add yolk of the above egg, ½ teaspoon salt, and monosodium glutamate. Fry into 3 flat sheets 8″ square and cut off ends to square. Add carrots to ⅔ of the crab meat and mix well. Place a 28″ bamboo mat, similar to a miniature venetian blind on the table and spread a cloth on it. Place the three fried egg sheets on the cloth with edges overlapping. Make a paste of egg white and 1 teaspoon cornstarch and brush over all the egg sheets, particularly under the overlapping edges. Divide the crab meat mixed with carrot into halves and spread on the left side and right side egg sheets. Spread the center sheet with the crab meat without carrot. Roll in from both sides until the two rolls meet at the center. Brush with the egg white and cornstarch paste where the rolls meet. Roll in cloth and steam for 15 minutes. Cool and cut in rings of ½″ thickness before serving. Serve cold. *Serves 2–3.*

JELLIED CHICKEN

Chi Tung

A Shantung dish, introduced to the imperial court during the Ming period. It is delicious in the summer as a cold dish served with wine.

½ pound pork skin, hair removed and the skin washed (a package of stock aspic may be substituted)
10 cups water
1" cube ginger root, crushed, and ½" cube ginger root
2 teaspoons licorice root (place each teaspoon in a cloth bag)
4 2" long pieces green onion
5 pounds poulard in 1" cubes
1½ tablespoons salt or more to suit taste
2 tablespoons wine

Place the pork skin in a pot with 6 cups water, 1" ginger cube crushed, 1 bag licorice, and 1 piece onion. Bring to a boil over high heat uncovered, then lower the heat to medium and boil until the stock is reduced to 3 cups, about 2 or more hours. Discard the pork skin and bag of licorice, strain the stock, and pour into a pot. Stew the chicken cubes in 4 cups water with ½" ginger cube, a bag of licorice, and 3 pieces onion. Bring to a boil over high heat covered, then reduce the heat to low and simmer for 2 hours. Drain the chicken stock and save for other purpose. Place the chicken cubes in the pot of pork stock. Add salt and wine, bring to a boil over high heat uncovered. Lower heat to moderate and cook for 10 minutes. Place the chicken and the stock into a deep dish. Cool and refrigerate until jellied. Invert the bowl of jellied chicken onto a platter before serving. Serve chilled. *Serves 6–8.*

JELLIED FISH

Yü Tung

½ *pound pork skin, hair removed and the skin washed (a package of stock aspic may be substituted)*

8 cups water

2 1″ ginger roots cubed and 1″ ginger root, crushed

2 teaspoons licorice root (place each teaspoon in a cloth bag)

4 2″ long pieces green onion

2 carp, ½ pound each, scaled, cleaned, washed in salt water, heads and tails removed, and cut in 1″ lengths

3 tablespoons soy

1 teaspoon salt

1 tablespoon wine

Place the pork skin in a pot with 6 cups water, 1″ ginger cube, crushed, 1 bag licorice and 1 piece onion. Bring to a boil over high heat uncovered, then lower the heat to medium and boil until the stock is reduced to 3 cups, or about 2 or more hours. Discard the pork skin and the bag of licorice, strain the stock, and pour into a pot. Place the pieces of fish in a pot with 2 cups of water, 3 pieces onion, crushed ginger, 1 bag licorice, and soy. Bring to a boil uncovered for 20 minutes. Drain. Place pieces of fish in the pot of pork stock and add salt and wine. Bring to a boil over high heat uncovered, lower the heat to moderate, and simmer for 10 minutes. Place the fish and the pork stock in a deep dish. Cool and refrigerate until jellied. Invert the bowl of jellied fish onto a platter before serving. Serve chilled. *Serves 4–6.*

PORK KIDNEY WITH SAUCE

Pan Yao P'ien

Another favorite Shantung dish.

2 tablespoons green onion, chopped
2 teaspoons ginger root, chopped
3 tablespoons soy
½ teaspoon salt
1 tablespoon vinegar
1 tablespoon wine
1 tablespoon peppercorn oil (see page 37)
3 pork kidneys (see page 37), sliced

Combine ginger, soy, salt, vinegar, wine, and pepper-corn oil in a bowl. Place kidney slices in a sieve and pour boiling water over them until parboiled and whitened. Place in a deep dish and, just before serving, mix kidney slices with the sauce. Serve cold. *Serves 4–5.*

PORK LIVER COOKED WITH FIVE SPICES

Wu Hsiang Chu Kan

Manchurians used to sacrifice hogs on festivals twice a year in spring and fall. Every portion of the hog was cooked in a simple style. Liver, boiled in salt water, was called Yen Fa Chu Kan. Wu Hsiang Chu Kan was devised after the Manchurians entered the mainland of China.

1 pound pork liver, thoroughly washed
4 cups water
3 tablespoons soy
1 tablespoon wine
1 teaspoon sugar
1 teaspoon Five Spices

Bring to a boil 3 cups water in a pot, put in the washed liver, and boil for 30 minutes. Empty the water from the pot in which the liver was cooked and add soy, wine, sugar, Five Spices, and 1 cup of fresh water. Simmer over low heat for 1 hour. Remove the liver from the pot, wipe away any liquid with a cloth, and cut in 2″ × 1″ × 1/8″ slices. Serve cold. This recipe is especially good to serve as hors d'oeuvres. *Serves 3–4.*

SWEET, SOUR, AND HOT CHINESE CABBAGE

T'ang Ts'u La Pai Ts'ai

2 tablespoons sesame oil
3/4 pound Chinese cabbage, tenderest part, in 1½" cubes
2 tablespoons sugar
1 tablespoon vinegar
2 tablespoons soy
2 cayenne peppers, julienned

Bring sesame oil to a boil in a large iron pan, put in Chinese cabbage, and fry 1 minute. Add sugar, vinegar, and soy. Cook, while stirring, for 2 minutes or more, add peppers, and fry 1 more minute. Remove pan from fire, place cabbage in a deep bowl, and serve cold. *Serves 2–3.*

SOUPS

CHICKEN, BAMBOO, AND MUSHROOM SOUP

Chi P'ien Sun P'ien Kou Mo T'ang

1 ½ tablespoons green onion, julienned
¼" cube ginger root, crushed
¾ cup bamboo shoots, julienned
½ pound chicken fillet, julienned
4 dried mushrooms (see page 36) in 1" × ¼" pieces (save stock)
2 cups chicken stock (see page 41)
1 cup mushroom stock (see above)
2 tablespoons soy
1 teaspoon salt
½ teaspoon monosodium glutamate
1 tablespoon wine

Place in a medium-sized bowl ingredients in the following sequence: onion and ginger on the bottom, bamboo shoots, chicken fillet and mushrooms on top. Pour chicken and mushroom stocks over ingredients. Add soy, salt, monosodium glutamate, and wine. Place in a steamer and steam for 30 minutes. Serve hot. *Serves 3–4.*

CHICKEN, SHRIMP, AND VEGETABLE SOUP

San Hsien T'ang

This was originally a Shantung dish but is found every-
where today.

4 cups chicken stock (see page 41)
1½ tablespoons green onion, julienned
1 teaspoon ginger root, julienned
¼ cup dried mushrooms (see page 36), julienned
2 tablespoons soy
½ teaspoon salt
¼ pound chicken fillet, julienned
¼ pound fresh shrimp, 2" length, shelled, deveined, and
    washed
4 snowpeas, julienned

Bring the chicken stock to a boil in a pot, and add other
ingredients. Bring to a boil. Serve hot. *Serves 4.*

CHINESE CABBAGE SOUP

Pai Ts'ai T'ang

The best Chinese cabbage is produced in Shantung and here is a Shantung recipe for cabbage soup.

2 tablespoons lard, rendered
1 cup dried shrimp (see page 38)
1 tablespoon green onion, julienned
½ tablespoon ginger root, sliced
1 pound Chinese cabbage, tenderest part, cut in 1½" cubes
4 cups sparerib stock (see page 42)
1 teaspoon salt or more if necessary

Heat the lard in a pot and fry shrimp, onion, ginger, and Chinese cabbage, stirring well, for 10 minutes. Pour in sparerib stock and simmer over low heat covered for 20 minutes or more until the Chinese cabbage becomes tender. Add salt and stir. Simmer for 3 minutes uncovered. Serve hot. This soup may be reheated. *Serves 4–5.*

CHRYSANTHEMUM AND CHICKEN SOUP

Chü Hua Chi T'ang

Although chrysanthemums are obtainable at any time of the year nowadays, this dish in the olden days was enjoyed as a seasonal dish in the fall.

5 cups chicken stock (see page 41)
1/4 pound chicken fillet, julienned
1 1/2 teaspoons salt or more to suit taste
1/2 teaspoon monosodium glutamate
5 fresh white chrysanthemums, small, petals only (see page 35)

Bring the chicken stock to a boil in a pot and add chicken meat, salt, and monosodium glutamate. Bring to a boil again and place in a large soup bowl. Sprinkle with petals and serve at once. Serve hot. This soup must be served immediately after the chrysanthemum petals have been added or they will become bitter. *Serves 5.*

HAM AND MARROW SOUP

Huo Jou Tung Kua T'ang

Originally a Chiangnan dish, this was introduced to the court during the reign of Emperor Ch'ien-lung.

1 tablespoon green onion julienned
¼ teaspoon ginger root, julienned
½ cup dried shrimp (see page 38)
½ cup marrow (see page 36), cut in 1″ × ½″ × ⅓″ pieces,
*   cooked for 10 minutes in 2 cups water, and drained.*
½ cup ham, julienned
3 cups clear chicken stock (see page 41)
1 teaspoon salt

Place at the bottom of a bowl onion, ginger root, and shrimp. Lay marrow neatly over them, place ham on top of marrow, and add chicken stock. Steam for 30 minutes at high temperature. Do not overcook marrow or the flavor of the ham will not penetrate. Serve hot. *Serves 4–5.*

HOT AND SOUR CUTTLEFISH SOUP

Yü Yü Suan La T'ang

This famous Honan dish is said to have a sobering effect when taken after excessive drinking.

2 cups carp, cut in irregular pieces

5 cups abalone stock (see page 43)

½ cup dried shrimp (see page 38)

2 dried cuttlefish (see page 33) about 10″ × 6″, sliced in 1″ × ½″ pieces

½ cup bamboo shoots (see page 33), cut aslant in 1″ × ½″ pieces

½ cup celery, cut aslant in 1″ pieces, boiled for 10 minutes and drained

4 tablespoons soy

2 tablespoons vinegar

1 teaspoon black pepper

Add the carp to the abalone stock in a pot and bring to a boil uncovered over high heat. Add shrimp and cook 3 minutes. Add cuttlefish, bamboo shoots, and celery, and cook for 3 minutes. Season with soy, vinegar, and pepper, stir well, and cook uncovered for another 3 minutes. Serve hot. This is a delicious fish chowder. *Serves 5–6.*

PICKLED VEGETABLE ROOT SOUP

Cha Ts'ai T'ang

Although this was originally a Soochow dish, it was brought over through Shantung and introduced to the imperial court of Ming toward the end of their dynasty.

5 cups sparerib stock (see page 42)
¼ cup vegetable root, pickled (see page 232), in 1" × ¼" × ⅛" pieces
1½ tablespoons green onion, julienned
1 teaspoon ginger root, julienned
¼ pound pork, julienned
1¼ cups bamboo shoots (see page 33), julienned
2 tablespoons soy
¼ teaspoon red pepper

Bring the sparerib stock to a boil in a pot, add pickles, and cook 10 minutes. Add onion and ginger, bring to a boil, and then add pork, bamboo shoots, soy, and pepper. Cook until the pork is thoroughly done. Stir well. Serve hot. *Serves 5.*

RIVER BALL SOUP

Chuan Wan Tzu

¾ pound pork, chopped
1 egg white
2 tablespoons green onion, julienned
1½ tablespoons soy
1½ teaspoons salt
1 tablespoon sesame oil
1 tablespoon cornstarch
2 cups marrow (see page 36), julienned
4 cups chicken stock (see page 41)
¼ teaspoon monosodium glutamate

Mix pork with egg white, onion, soy, 1 teaspoon salt, sesame oil, and cornstarch. Form into balls ½″ diameter. Boil marrow in chicken stock uncovered over high heat until translucent. Add meat balls, ½ teaspoon salt, and monosodium glutamate. Lower heat to medium and simmer uncovered for 3 to 4 minutes until meat balls are well done. Serve hot. *Serves 4.*

SWALLOWS' NEST CLEAR SOUP

Ch'ing T'ang Yen Ts'ai

4 swallows' nests (see page 38)
½ cup Chinese ham (julienned)
2 quarts clear chicken stock (see page 41)
1 tablespoon salt
1 tablespoon wine
2 teaspoons monosodium glutamate

Steep swallows' nests in 2½ cups warm chicken stock for 30 minutes. Drain. Put Chinese ham in 5½ cups chicken stock and add salt and wine. Bring to a boil over high heat uncovered. Put in drained swallows' nests and sprinkle with monosodium glutamate and bring to a boil. Serve hot. *Serves 7–8.*

Chinese table setting

Ta lu sauce with noodles

Fried soybean paste sauce with noodles

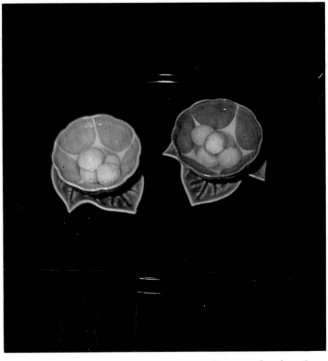

Rice powder dumplings

Steamed bean curd in a casserole

Hot and sour cuttlefish soup

Chrysanthemum and chicken soup

Jellied chicken

Clear chicken soup with jasmine

Fried bananas

Chicken cooked with bean curd

Miniature dumpling with filling

Lotus root stuffed with glutinous rice

Braised bamboo shoots with soy

Spinach with sauce

Pork kidney and bean curd skin

Soochow style dish

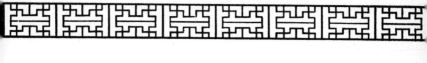

CASSEROLES
AND
CHAFING DISHES

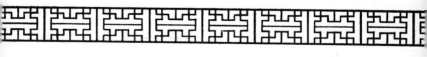

BEAN CURD CASSEROLE

Tou Fu Kuo

This well-known Chiangnan dish was introduced to the imperial court during the reign of Emperor Ch'ien-lung.

¾ *pound bean curd*
1 tablespoon pork fat in ½" cubes
½ cup Chinese ham, julienned
4 fresh prawns, 4" long, shelled and deveined
2 tablespoons dried shrimp (see page 38)
2 teaspoons green onion, chopped
1 teaspoon ginger root, chopped
2 medium-sized dried mushrooms (see page 36), julienned
½ cup bamboo shoots (see page 33), julienned
4½ to 5 cups chicken stock (see page 41)
2 teaspoons salt or more to suit taste

Place the bean curd in the center of a large casserole, preferably flat, and dot with pork fat. Around the bean curd, place ham, prawns, shrimp, onion, ginger, mushrooms, and bamboo shoots. Add chicken stock and salt. Cover and steam over high heat for ½ hour. Serve hot. *Serves 2–3.*

PHEASANT CASSEROLE

Yeh Chi Kuo

This is a Manchurian dish. A great number of pheasants thrive in pine forests of Manchuria where they feed on pine seeds and become fat and tender.

1 teaspoon green onion, chopped

1 teaspoon ginger root, chopped

3 tablespoons soy

2 tablespoons sesame paste (see page 38)

1 teaspoon shrimp sauce

1 teaspoon red pepper oil (see page 37)

3 pheasants, 3 pounds each, boned and cut in 2″ × 1″ by ⅛″ slices

4½ cups water or more if needed

4 ounces vegetable greens, pickled (see page 232), washed, drained, and chopped

3 tablespoons pine seeds (see page 37)

1 tablespoon lard

4 ounces bean curd, dried (see page 34), cut in 1″ × ½″ × ½″ pieces

Combine onion, ginger root, soy, sesame paste, shrimp sauce, and red pepper oil in a bowl and mix well into a sauce. Arrange slices of pheasants attractively on a platter and place on the table.

Pour 4½ cups water in the chafing dish and cover. Light and, when water comes to a boil, add pickled vegetable greens, pine seeds, and lard. Bring to a boil again and add dried bean curd and let come to a boil. Place the chafing dish in the middle of the table. Add pheasant slices and bring to a boil. Put prepared sauce into the chafing dish, stir well, and reduce heat. Guests serve themselves from the chafing dish. The broth is served in individual bowls to each guest. *Serves 4–5.*

BROCADE-LIKE ARRAY OF CHICKEN, PORK, PRAWNS, AND VEGETABLES

Shih Chin Huo Kuo

This is a southern Chinese dish which was introduced long ago to the imperial court. It was enjoyed as part of the New Year's feast.

1 pound chicken, dressed

6 cups water

3¼ teaspoons salt

4 pieces green onion, cut aslant in 1″ lengths

¼″ cubed ginger root, chopped, and ¼″ cubed ginger root, sliced

¼ pound pork, lean and fat, chopped

⅛ teaspoon pepper

½ tablespoon cornstarch

1 cup sesame oil

2 pieces dried sea cucumbers (see page 37)

¼ pound fresh prawns 4″ long, shelled and deveined

¼ pound Chinese cabbage, cut in 1″ × ½″ × ½″ pieces

¼ cup bamboo shoots (see page 33), julienned

1 cup Chinese vermicelli, steeped in hot water for 10 minutes and drained

2 medium-sized dried mushrooms (see page 36), julienned

½ pound pork kidney (see page 37), cut in 1″ × ½″ × ¼″ pieces

¼ pound Chinese ham, steamed for 1 hour, julienned. If plain boiled ham is substituted, it does not require steaming.

5½ cups chicken stock, including 1 cup for replenishing (see page 41)

¼ cup soy

¼ cup vinegar

Place the chicken in a pot and pour in water. Add 2 teaspoons salt, 2 pieces onion, and sliced ginger. Boil uncovered for 1 hour over moderate heat. Remove the chicken from the pot, tear off the chicken meat with fingers, and cut in $1'' \times \frac{1}{2}'' \times \frac{1}{2}''$ pieces.

Mix with chopped pork $\frac{1}{4}$ teaspoon salt, pepper, and cornstarch and form into $1''$ diameter balls. Heat sesame oil in a pan and fry the meat balls until light brown.

Place chicken, onion, ginger, fried pork balls, sea cucumbers, prawns, cabbage, bamboo shoots, vermicelli, mushrooms, kidney, and ham attractively on platters which will surround the chafing dish when it is placed in the center of the table.

Put in the chafing dish $4\frac{1}{2}$ cups of chicken stock, and add 2 pieces of onion and chopped ginger. Cover and light chafing dish. Bring to a boil and place the chafing dish in the middle of the table. Uncover and add small bits of the ingredients from the platters in the sequence mentioned above and bring to a boil. Serve and continue adding the ingredients as needed. Replenish chicken stock and salt if necessary.

This dish may be reheated. Guests help themselves from the chafing dish and use the soy and vinegar, served in saucers, to season to taste. The stock is poured into individual bowls placed on the table for each guest. *Serves 4–5.*

CHRYSANTHEMUM CASSEROLE

Chü Hua Kuo Tzu

One of the favorite pastimes of the emperor was to dine with friends under a full August moon, enjoying the rich broth and delicious morsels prepared in a charcoal chafing dish.

$2\frac{1}{2}$ *quarts chicken stock, including* $4\frac{1}{2}$ *cups for replenishing (see page 41)*

3 teaspoons salt

$\frac{1}{2}$ *cup green onion, cut aslant in 1" pieces*

1 tablespoon dried shrimp (see page 38)

3 dried scallops (see page 37)

12 pieces dried bean curd (see page 34)

$\frac{3}{4}$ *pound bean curd, cut in* $1" \times \frac{1}{2}" \times \frac{1}{2}"$ *pieces*

$\frac{1}{2}$ *pound Chinese vermicelli:* $\frac{1}{4}$ *pound steeped in hot water and drained;* $\frac{1}{4}$ *pound deep-fried in 2 cups vegetable oil*

$\frac{1}{2}$ *pound fillet of chicken, sliced in* $1" \times \frac{1}{2}" \times \frac{1}{2}"$ *pieces*

6 pieces Chinese doughnuts (see page 34), cut in $\frac{1}{2}"$ *pieces*

$\frac{1}{2}$ *pound fillet of white flesh fish, sliced in* $1" \times \frac{1}{2}" \times \frac{1}{2}"$ *pieces*

10 small white chrysanthemums, petals only (if dried, see page 35)

$\frac{1}{2}$ *cup soy*

$\frac{1}{2}$ *cup vinegar*

Make an attractive arrangement of onions, shrimp, scallops, dried bean curd, bean curd, Chinese vermicelli, both steeped and fried, chicken, Chinese doughnuts, fish, and chrysanthemums on platters which will surround the chafing dish when it is placed in the center of the table.

Fill the chafing dish with 4½ cups chicken stock, add 2 teaspoons salt and cover. Light chafing dish and when the stock begins to boil, place chafing dish in the middle of the table. Uncover and add small portions of all ingredients from the platters in the above-named sequence except chrysanthemum petals which are added after all the other ingredients come to a boil.

Overcooked chrysanthemum petals turn bitter. If the chafing dish becomes too hot, reduce heat. Guests help themselves from the chafing dish and use the vinegar and soy, served in saucers, to season to taste. The stock is poured into individual bowls placed on the table for each guest. Continue adding ingredients as needed. Replenish the chicken stock and salt if necessary. *Serves 3–4.*

EIGHT FAIRIES CASSEROLE

Pa Hsien Kuo

The charming name of Eight Fairies was given to this casserole just for amusement. The eight main ingredients: chicken, Chinese cabbage, sea cucumbers, shark's fin, dove eggs, mushroom, Chinese ham and prawns represent the fairies.

5 pounds chicken, dressed
3 tablespoons salt or more to suit taste
3 teaspoons peppercorns
2 cardamon seeds
8 2" long pieces green onion
2 pieces ginger root, in 1" cubes
1 pound Chinese cabbage, leaves separated, washed, and drained
5 dried sea cucumbers (see page 37)
1 tablespoon dried shrimp (see page 38). Save stock.
2 processed shark's fins (see page 38)
15 dove eggs, boiled and shelled (see page 35)
10 dried mushrooms (see page 36), julienned. Save stock.
1 pound Chinese ham, julienned
1 teaspoon monosodium glutamate
20 fresh prawns, shelled, deveined, and washed
3 tablespoons wine

Place the chicken in a pot and pour in enough water to cover. Add 1½ tablespoons salt, peppercorns, cardamon, onion, and ginger. Bring to a boil, then lower the heat and simmer covered for 1¼ hours.

Remove the chicken from the pot, tear off chicken meat with fingers, and slice into 1″ × ½″ × ½″ pieces. Save stock for later use.

Lay the Chinese cabbage evenly in a large earthenware casserole. Put in chicken meat, sea cucumbers, dried shrimp, shark's fin, dove eggs, mushrooms, and Chinese ham. Pour in stocks of mushrooms, shrimp, and enough chicken stock to cover the ingredients. Add 1½ table-spoons salt, monosodium glutamate, and wine. Simmer covered over low heat for 45 minutes, then add fresh prawns. Bring to a boil, uncovered. Stir carefully but well. Serve hot. *Serves 10–12*.

EXCELLENT CASSEROLE

Yi P'ing Kuo

This dish was carried over into the imperial court of Ching from the Ming period, and it was used as a gift from the emperor to his consort or to the empress dowager. After it was introduced to the public, it was used as a gift to relatives in the springtime.

5 pounds chicken, dressed
4 tablespoons salt or more if needed
1 teaspoon peppercorns
4 water chestnuts, washed
8 tablespoons wine
5 pounds duck, dressed, feet removed, legs bent and tied to the body with strings
6 1½" long pieces green onion
¾" cubed ginger root, crushed
3 tablespoons lard
1 tablespoon green onion, chopped
1 tablespoon ginger root, chopped
1 pound Chinese cabbage, cut in 1" cubes
2 tablespoons dried shrimp (see page 38)
5 cups chicken stock (see page 41)
15 dove eggs, boiled and shelled (see page 35)
4 dried sea cucumbers (see page 37)
2½ pounds Chinese ham, julienned
1½ pounds processed shark's fins (see page 38)
1 teaspoon monosodium glutamate

Place the chicken in a pot with the breast down and fill the pot with enough water to cover the chicken. Add 1½ tablespoons salt, peppercorns, water chestnuts, and 3 tablespoons wine. After bringing the chicken to a boil once, simmer covered for 2 hours over low heat. Remove chicken, strain and reserve 5 cups stock. In a separate pot, place the duck with enough water to cover and add 5 tablespoons wine, 6 pieces onion, and ¾″ cubed ginger, crushed. Cook covered 2 hours over high heat until very tender and add 1½ tablespoons salt.

Heat the lard in a pan, add chopped onion, chopped ginger, dried shrimp, Chinese cabbage, and 1 tablespoon salt. Pour in enough chicken stock to cover the ingredients and cook until the cabbage becomes tender.

Lay the cabbage evenly in the center of a large earthenware or any large flat casserole. Arrange around the cabbage dove eggs, sea cucumbers, Chinese ham, and shark's fin. Place in the center on the cabbage the boiled duck, untied, and the boiled chicken. Place water chestnuts alongside of the duck. Pour in enough chicken stock to cover the lower half of the duck and chicken, sprinkle with 1 teaspoon of monosodium glutamate and place the casserole in a steamer and steam 1 hour. Remove from the steamer. Serve hot in the casserole. *Serves 10–12.*

MUTTON CASSEROLE

Yang Jou Shua Kuo

This is another dish the Manchurians brought to China. It was customarily taken on the first day of winter in the court.

4 tablespoons soy

2 tablespoons sesame paste (see page 38)

2 cubes fermented bean curd (use fu ju see page 34)

2 tablespoons leek flower, salted (see page 36)

1½ tablespoons shrimp sauce

1½ tablespoons red pepper oil (see page 37)

5 tablespoons coriander, chopped. Place 2 tablespoons in a saucer and use the rest for replenishing. (Lettuce or Chinese cabbage may be substituted.)

1½ tablespoons ginger root, chopped

2 tablespoons green onion, chopped

2 garlic cloves, candied (see page 35), quartered

½ cup turnip tops, pickled, washed, drained, and chopped

½ teaspoon lard

2 pounds mutton cut in 2″ × 1″ × ⅛″ slices (Prime ribs of beef may be substituted)

1 cup soured Chinese cabbage, washed, drained, and cut in 2″ × 1″ strips (see page 232)

½ cup Chinese vermicelli, steeped in hot water for 10 minutes and drained

6 pieces bean curd dried (see page 34), cut in 1″ × ½″ × ½″ pieces

4½ cups water. Replenish if necessary.

Put soy, sesame paste, fermented bean curd, salted leek flowers, shrimp sauce, red pepper oil, coriander, ginger, onion, and candied garlic into 10 separate little dishes and place them on the side of the table. Each guest may prepare his own sauce by combining the 9 different ingredients; the candied garlic is optional.

Arrange mutton, soured Chinese cabbage, vermicelli, and dried bean curd attractively on platters which will surround the chafing dish when it is placed in the center of the table.

Fill the chafing dish with 4½ cups of water, put in chopped turnip tops and lard, and cover. Light the chafing dish and when the stock comes to a boil, place the chafing dish in the middle of the table. Put in many slices of mutton and, after it has come to a boil for a few seconds and the soup has become somewhat thick, add small portions of soured Chinese cabbage, vermicelli, and dried bean curd. Bring to a boil. Continue adding the ingredients as needed. Replenish water if necessary. Guests help themselves from the chafing dish and use the sauce to season to taste. The broth which is delicious is poured into individual bowls placed on the table for each guest. *Serves 3–4.*

WATER SHIELD CASSEROLE

Shun Kuo

Emperor Ch'ien-lung favored this dish. It was originally from Hangchow where water shields are produced.

2 tablespoons green onion, julienned
$\frac{1}{4}$" cube ginger root, julienned
$\frac{1}{2}$ pound chicken meat, julienned
1 pound mandarin fish (see page 36), cut in $\frac{1}{2}$" × 1" × $\frac{1}{8}$" pieces, skinned and boned
2 pork kidneys (see page 37), cut in 1" × $\frac{1}{2}$" × $\frac{1}{8}$" pieces
$\frac{1}{2}$ cup water shields (see page 39), washed
$6\frac{1}{2}$ cups chicken stock, including 2 cups for replenishing (see page 41)
$1\frac{1}{2}$ teaspoons salt or more to suit taste
$\frac{1}{4}$ cup soy
$\frac{1}{4}$ cup vinegar

Arrange onion, ginger root, chicken, fish, kidneys, and water shields attractively on plates which will surround the chafing dish when it is placed in the center of the table. Pour $4\frac{1}{2}$ cups chicken stock into the chafing dish and add $1\frac{1}{2}$ teaspoons salt and cover. Light chafing dish and, when the stock comes to a boil, place the chafing dish in the center of the table. Uncover and add small bits of ingredients from the plates in the above-mentioned sequence. Reduce heat if the chafing dish becomes too hot. Guests help themselves and use vinegar and soy, served in saucers, to season to taste. The stock is served in individual bowls to each guest. Add ingredients as needed. Replenish stock and salt if necessary. *Serves 2–3.*

SNACK

SNACKS

Tien Hsin

Tien hsin means a snack or something to be eaten between meals. China used to have a large variety of snacks, many of which have their particular traditions and legends. *Man t'ou,* a kind of a steamed bread of North China, is an example. During the San Kuo period when Chi Ke Lian came to the River Lu Shui on his way home after having conquered Mongolia, many ghosts of the dead soldiers appeared and blocked the road and prevented his army from crossing the river. He learned that the local tradition was to offer 49 human heads to console the dead. But the battle was over and there was nobody to kill. Therefore, the general ordered that dough be made into the shape of human heads and steamed and that these be offered to the souls of the dead. The general's idea turned out to be a success for his army crossed the river safely. Whether it is true or not this legend is well-known.

During the reign of Emperors K'ang-hsi and Ch'ien-lung when China was peaceful and rich, tasty and elegant dishes were perfected. The *tien hsin* of the court were mostly from Kwantung (Canton) and Yangchou (near Nanking), but were improved upon by the pastry cooks of the imperial kitchen.

Tien hsin as well as dinners were given to princes and ministers on every annual festival. Gradually, their cooks began to imitate the *tien hsin* of the court. The most famous were *niu yu po,* "butter" bun, of which there were hundreds of kinds prepared at the palace of Prince Yü, and fruit *tien hsin* at the palace of Prince Hsiao, both of whom were kinsmen of the emperor. Later some of these cooks opened *tien hsin* shops in the city and, if they won a reputation and the store became famous, a member of the family sometimes gained the position of a eunuch in the imperial palace.

On the following pages will be found various kinds of snacks, all of which are easily prepared. They are divided into categories: dumplings with filling, pancakes, porridge, noodles, steamed breads, and miscellaneous snacks.

DUMPLINGS WITH FILLINGS

Tai Hsien

Tai hsien is a kind of pastry-type snack, consisting of a "doily" of pastry with a filling made of vegetables, sea food, or meat. Hundreds of kinds were made at the court, but only three are included here: stuffed dumplings, miniature stuffed dumplings, pancakes, and stuffed pancakes. The term "doily" means the small, thin outer skin made of rolled dough which is filled and cooked. In preparing stuffed dumplings there are four steps to be considered: making the dough, rolling the doily pastry, making the filling, and the cooking method (boiling, steaming, or poaching). Dumplings are seasoned individually to taste with soy and vinegar.

BOILED DUMPLINGS (40 pieces)

Chiao Tzu

(1) Place 1½ cups sifted flour and ½ cup water in a bowl, mix well, and knead until smooth. Cover with a wet cloth and let stand for 30 minutes. Form a roll 15″ long and 1″ in diameter and cut into ½″ pieces. Roll and press flat on lightly floured board with a rolling pin to form round doilies 3″ diameter. (2) Place 1 heaping teaspoon filling in the center of each piece. Fold in half and seal edge. (3) Fill a pot 10″ deep and 15″ diameter ¾ full of water and bring to a boil. Put in dumplings, bring to a boil uncovered, add 1 cup water, and bring to a boil again uncovered. Remove dumplings and serve hot. Deep-fried dumplings after they have been boiled and cooled are also delicious.

STEAMED DUMPLINGS

Cheng Chiao Tzu

(1) Place 1½ cups sifted flour and ½ cup hot water in a bowl and mix well. Then knead until smooth. Cover with a wet cloth and let stand for 30 minutes. (2) Follow Step 2 above. (3) Spread a cloth on the bottom of steaming basket and put in dumplings. Place steaming basket over boiling water and steam for 20 minutes. Serve hot.

POACHED DUMPLINGS

Kuo T'ieh Chiao Tzu

(1) Follow Step 1 for Steamed Dumplings. (2) Follow Step 2 for Boiled Dumplings. (3) Heat 2 tablespoons oil over low heat in a pan, bring to a boil, and spread well. Stand dumplings in rows and brown over moderate heat. Then pour in enough water to submerge ⅓ of dumplings. Reduce heat to low and poach until hardly any water remains. Scoop out dumplings and serve hot.

FILLINGS FOR DUMPLINGS

SHRIMP AND SEA CUCUMBER FILLING

San Hsien Hsien

4 medium-sized dried mushrooms (see page 36), chopped
½ pound fresh shrimp, shelled, deveined, chopped
8 pieces dried sea cucumbers (see page 37), chopped
2 tablespoons green onion, chopped
1 tablespoon ginger root, chopped
2 tablespoons soy or more to suit taste
½ tablespoon monosodium glutamate
2 tablespoons sesame oil

Place all ingredients in a bowl and mix well. Let stand 20 minutes before filling dumplings.

CHINESE CABBAGE AND PORK FILLING

Pai Ts'ai Chu Jou Hsien

½ pound pork, chopped

4 tablespoons green onion, chopped

2 tablespoons ginger root, chopped

2 tablespoons soy

½ pound Chinese cabbage, chopped fine, wrapped in a cloth
  and pressed to remove water

½ teaspoon salt or more to suit taste

½ teaspoon monosodium glutamate

2 tablespoons sesame oil

Place all ingredients in a bowl and mix well. Let stand
for 20 minutes before filling dumplings.

CRAB MEAT FILLING

Hsieh Jou Hsien

½ pound crab meat, fresh or canned, bones removed

3 tablespoons green onion, chopped

2 tablespoons ginger root, chopped

½ cup bamboo shoots (see page 33), chopped

4 medium-sized dried mushrooms (see page 36), chopped

1 tablespoon soy

1 tablespoon wine

½ teaspoon salt or more to suit taste

½ teaspoon monosodium glutamate

2 tablespoons sesame oil

Place all ingredients in a bowl and mix well. Let stand 20
minutes before filling dumplings.

MINIATURE DUMPLINGS (80 pieces)

Hun Tun

In addition to doily and filling, miniature dumplings are served with soup and seasoning. The boiled and drained dumplings are placed in individual bowls of stock and served hot with special seasonings. (1) Place 1 cup sifted flour and ⅓ cup water in a bowl, mix well, and knead. Cover with wet cloth and let stand 30 minutes. Form a roll 10″ long and 1″ diameter and slice into ½″ pieces. Roll and press with rolling pin until paper thin. Form into doilies 5″ diameter and then quarter. (2) Place ¼ teaspoon filling in the center of each fan-shaped doily and fold it toward the circular arc. Seal edge and bring folded ends together. Stand the miniature dumplings with the two ends up. (3) Follow Step 3 for Boiled dumplings. (4) Drain. Like boiled dumplings, these miniature dumplings may be cooled and deep-fried to make wonderful hors d'oeuvres. In China, each dumpling is identified by the name of the filling which is marked on the dumpling.

FILLINGS FOR MINIATURE DUMPLINGS

PORK FILLING

Chen Jou Hsien

4 ounces pork, chopped
½ teaspoon ginger root, chopped
1 tablespoon green onion, chopped
¼ teaspoon salt

Place ingredients in a bowl and let stand for 20 minutes before filling dumplings.

CHICKEN AND MUSHROOM FILLING

Chi Jou Kou Mo Hsien

4 ounces chicken meat, chopped
4 medium-sized dried mushrooms (see page 36), chopped
1 tablespoon green onion, chopped
¼ teaspoon ginger root, chopped
1 tablespoon soy
¼ teaspoon salt
1 tablespoon sesame oil

Place ingredients in a bowl and let stand for 20 minutes before filling dumplings.

SHRIMP AND SEA CUCUMBER FILLING

San Hsien Hsien

See page 195. Use half portion.

SPARERIB STOCK FOR MINIATURE DUMPLINGS

Che Ku T'ang

1 pound spareribs
1 4" long piece green onion
2 pieces ginger root, in ½" cubes, crushed
½ tablespoon salt or more to suit taste
¼ teaspoon monosodium glutamate

Place spareribs in a large pot, add twice as much water as spareribs in volume. Add other ingredients. Bring to a boil and simmer over low heat uncovered for 1 hour. Chicken stock (see page 41) may also be used.

SEASONING FOR MINIATURE DUMPLINGS

Hsiang Liao

½ cup coriander, julienned (Chinese cabbage or other greens
  may be substituted.)
1 tablespoon dried shrimp (see page 38), chopped
2 sheets dried laver, 10" square, cut in 1½" strips
½ teaspoon black pepper

Before serving dumplings, sprinkle each bowl of dumplings with the above seasonings. Serve hot. *Serves 8.*

PANCAKES

Ping

Chinese pancakes in this form are similar to the Western type and, in the North where much flour is produced, they are a staple food. In the South where rice is the staple, pancakes are a kind of snack and are often served as a dessert. In the court various snacks were prepared for the emperor at every meal, and pancakes were indispensable. The pancakes made in the court were exquisite and were prepared by very special pastry cooks. Although there were many, many kinds, I am listing below four that are simple to make: family pancake, green onion pancake, spring pancake, and grated radish pancake.

FAMILY PANCAKES

Chia Chang Ping

2½ cups sifted flour
1 cup hot water
1⅓ tablespoons sesame oil for folding into pancakes plus 2⅔ tablespoons for frying
1 teaspoon salt

Put flour in a bowl, add hot water, and knead until smooth. Let stand 30 minutes. Form into a roll 8″ long and 2″ diameter. Cut into 1″ pieces and form a pocket in the center of each to contain ½ teaspoon sesame oil and 1/8 teaspoon salt. Fold sides gently toward center and knead well to mix the sesame oil and salt into the dough.

Pat into a round cake 2½″ diameter. Bring 1 teaspoon sesame oil to a boil in a frying pan over medium heat, spread well, and reduce heat to low. Fry each piece for 3 minutes, turning over frequently. Serve hot. *Serves 4.*

GREEN ONION PANCAKES

Tsung Hua Ping

2½ cups sifted flour
1 cup hot water
2⅔ tablespoons green onion, chopped
1⅓ tablespoons lard
1⅓ tablespoons sesame oil for frying
1 teaspoon salt

Put flour in a bowl, add hot water and knead until smooth. Let stand 30 minutes. Form into a roll of 8″ long and 2″ diameter. Cut into 1″ pieces and form a pocket in the center of each to contain ½ teaspoon lard, 1 teaspoon onion and 1/8 teaspoon salt. Fold sides gently towards the center and knead to mix well the lard, onion, and salt into the dough. Pat into a round cake of 2½″ diameter. Bring to a boil 1 teaspoon sesame oil in a frying pan over medium heat, spread well, and reduce heat to low. Fry each piece for 3 minutes, turning over frequently. Serve hot. *Serves 4.*

SPRING PANCAKES

Chung Ping

2½ cups sifted flour
2⅔ tablespoons seasame oil plus 1⅓ tablespoons for frying

Prepare the dough as directed in Green Onion Pancakes. Cut the dough into 1″ pieces and roll out thin round cakes of 4½″ diameter. Spread ½ teaspoon sesame oil over surface and cover with the second cake, similar to a sandwich. Repeat this process, stacking each pair on top of the preceding pair, like stacking hot cakes. Bring to a boil ½ teaspoon sesame oil in a frying pan over low heat and spread well. Fry each cake, turning frequently, until brown. Serve hot. *Serves 4.*

GRATED RADISH PANCAKES

Lo Pa Szu Ping

2 cups sifted flour
½ cup lard (*vegetable shortening may be substituted.*)
¾ cup water
¾ cup radish, grated, wrapped in a cloth, and pressed to remove water
2 tablespoons dried shrimp (*see page 38*), chopped
4 tablespoons green onion, chopped
¼ teaspoon salt
3 cups vegetable oil

In a bowl blend ¼ cup lard into the flour, add water, and gradually form a dough. Pat and roll out on a floured board. Dot the dough with 2 tablespoons lard. Dredge with flour, fold ends toward center, then double, pat and roll out and repeat until the lard is all used. Roll out the pastry into two 12″ squares.

In a bowl mix radish, shrimp, onion, and salt and spread pastry squares with the mixture. Roll the pastry to form a bar and seal the edges. Cut into 1″ cakes and even the cut ends. Bring vegetable oil to a boil, lower heat to medium, and deep-fry the cakes until they turn a light golden color. Serve hot or cold. *Serves 8–10.*

STUFFED PANCAKES

Hsien Ping

An unusual and delicious kind of pancake is the Stuffed Pancake described below. (1) Place 1½ cups of sifted flour and ½ cup of hot water in a bowl, mix well, and knead until smooth. Cover dough with a dampened cloth and let stand for 30 minutes. Form a roll 10″ long and 1″ diameter and cut into ½″ pieces. Roll and press with a rolling pin on a lightly floured board into flat pieces of 4″ diameter. (2) Place 1½ heaping teaspoons filling in the center of each piece of rolled dough and fold over. Place on a lightly floured pastry board and press lightly with a rolling pin into a flat round cake. (3) Bring to a boil 1 tablespoon oil in a flat bottomed pan over moderate heat. Spread oil and fry both sides of the cake until light brown. Serve hot. *Serves 10.*

FILLINGS FOR PANCAKES

MUTTON AND GREEN ONION FILLING

Yang Jou Tsung Hua Hsien

$\frac{1}{2}$ pound mutton, chopped
1 cup green onion, chopped
1 tablespoon ginger root, chopped
2 tablespoons sesame oil
1 tablespoon soy
$\frac{1}{4}$ teaspoon salt or more to suit taste

Place all ingredients in a bowl and mix well. Let stand for 20 minutes before filling pancakes.

MARROW AND PORK FILLING

Tung Kua Chu Jou Hsien

$\frac{1}{4}$ pound pork chopped
1 tablespoon green onion, chopped
1 teaspoon ginger root, chopped
2 tablespoons sesame oil
1 tablespoon soy
$\frac{1}{4}$ teaspoon salt or more to suit taste
$\frac{1}{4}$ pound marrow (see page 36), chopped, wrapped in a cloth, and pressed to remove water

Place all ingredients in a bowl and mix well. Let stand for 20 minutes before filling pancakes.

LEEK SPROUTS AND PORK FILLING

Chiu Huan Chu Jou Hsien

¼ *pound pork, chopped*
1 *teaspoon ginger root, chopped*
2 *tablespoons sesame oil*
1 *tablespoon soy*
¼ *teaspoon salt or more to suit taste*
¼ *pound leek sprout, chopped*

Place all ingredients except leek sprout in a bowl and mix well. Let stand for 20 minutes and then add leek sprout. Mix well before filling pancakes.

PORRIDGE

Chou

Chou, a porridge, was customarily taken after every meal in the court. Easily digested, it is considered a diet for the sick. Out of the many used, I am describing the preparation of four: Little Red Bean and Rice Porridge, Green Bean and Rice Porridge, La Pa Festival Porridge (consisting of fruits, nuts, beans, and rice), and Lotus Leaf and Rice Porridge. The green bean used here is not our familiar string been but the bean that is the source of bean sprouts (*liu tou*). *La pa* can be translated as ''harvest''.

LITTLE RED BEAN AND RICE PORRIDGE

Hung Tou Chou

1½ cups rice, washed
2 quarts plus 1½ cups water
¾ cup red beans, picked and washed

Place washed rice in a pot with 1½ quarts water and bring to a boil covered over high heat. Reduce the heat to low and simmer covered for 1 hour. Put red beans in another pot with 3½ cups water and bring to a boil covered over high heat. Reduce heat to low and simmer covered for 1 hour or until tender. Then combine rice and beans, stir well, and simmer covered over low heat for 20 minutes. Serve hot with sugar accompanied by pickles. This porridge is eaten in spring and winter. *Serves 10–12.*

LOTUS LEAF AND RICE PORRIDGE

He Yeh Chou

2 cups glutinous rice, soaked in water for 2 hours, washed and drained
3 quarts water
5 tender lotus leaves (see page 36)
30 lotus seeds (see page 36), sugared, cooked for ½ hour in 1½ cups water

Put rice and cooked lotus seeds in a large pot with water and bring to a boil covered. Reduce heat to low and put in lotus leaves and simmer uncovered for 1 hour. Remove leaves when the color and the fragrance have penetrated the rice. Serve soft rice in individual bowls and add sugar, if desired. Serve hot or cold. The fresh green color of the soft rice will change if the lotus leaves are left in the pot too long. This porridge is eaten in summer. *Serves 17–18.*

LA PA FESTIVAL PORRIDGE

La Pa Chou

1½ cups rice, washed
½ cup glutinous rice, washed
½ cup small red beans, picked and washed
10 dates, washed and seeded
2 tablespoons lotus seeds (sugared)
1 lily bulb, washed
2 tablespoons fresh noodles (packaged noodles may be substituted)
2 tablespoons raisins, washed and chopped
3 green plums, sugared, each cut in fifths
5 walnuts, shelled, blanched, and chopped
2 tablespoons watermelon seeds, shelled
3 dried haws (see page 36), chopped

Place in seaparate pots the following ingredients which require boiling. 1½ cups polished rice and ½ cup glutinous rice each with 3 quarts water and bring to a boil over high heat covered. Reduce heat to low and simmer covered for 1 hour. Put red beans in 3 cups water and bring to a boil over high heat covered. Reduce heat to low and simmer covered for 1 hour. Put dates in 2 cups water and bring to a boil over high heat covered. Reduce heat to low and simmer covered for ½ hour. Put lotus seeds in 1 cup water and bring to a boil over high heat covered. Reduce heat to low and simmer covered for ½ hour. Place a lily bulb in 1 cup water and bring to a boil over high heat covered. Reduce heat to low and simmer covered for 20 minutes. Put noodles in 2 cups water and bring to a boil over high heat uncovered. Lower heat and simmer for 10 minutes. If necessary, add more water. Combine all boiled ingredients in a pot and boil over low heat uncovered, stirring constantly, for 30 minutes. Serve in individual bowls garnished with raisins, plums, walnuts, watermelon seeds, and haws. Add sugar, if desired. Serve hot. This porridge was prepared for the Harvest Festival on December 8 which is comparable to the American Thanksgiving Day. *Serves 19–20.*

GREEN BEAN AND RICE PORRIDGE

Lü Tou Chou

2 cups rice, washed
1 gallon of water
½ cup green beans (liu tou), picked and washed

Place rice in a large pot with 3 quarts water and bring to a boil over high heat covered. Reduce heat to low and simmer covered for 1 hour. Place green beans in another pot with 1 quart water, bring to a boil over high heat covered. Reduce heat to low and simmer covered for 1 hour or more until tender. Then combine rice and green beans, stir well, and simmer over low heat covered for 20 minutes. Serve hot or cold with sugar accompanied by pickles. This porridge is eaten in summer and fall. *Serves 19–20.*

NOODLES

Mien T'iao

Mien t'iao is a staple food in the flour-producing North but is considered a snack in the South and in the court. Of the numerous kinds, here on the following pages will be found the method of making noodles along with various noodle recipes. These are divided into three types: noodles with stock, fried noodles, and noodles with sauce. If you prefer not to make noodle dough, commercially made noodles may be substituted.

NOODLE DOUGH

5 cups flour, not sifted
½ teaspoon salt
2 cups water

In a bowl mix flour, salt, and water and knead into a smooth dough. Cover with a wet cloth and let stand 20 minutes. Roll and press the dough on a flour dusted pastry board into a flat round sheet of 1/8″ thickness. Dust with flour, fold several times and cut into ribbons of about 1/8″ width. Dust with flour and separate the strips. Put strips in a kettle of hot boiling water and boil for 3 minutes. Strain and rinse in clear water and drain. *Serves 5.*

NOODLES WITH STOCK

T'ang Mien

JULIENNED CHICKEN MEAT WITH NOODLES

Chi Szu T'ang Mien

½ pound chicken meat boiled (see Shredded Chicken, page 85), julienned (fried chicken julienned may be substituted)
2½ tablespoons green onion, chopped
5 bowls boiled noodles
5 cups chicken stock, hot (see page 41)
1½ teaspoons salt or more to suit taste
½ teaspoon monosodium glutamate

Divide the chicken strips and chopped onion into 5 portions and add to 5 bowls of noodles. Pour over the noodles hot chicken stock seasoned with salt and monosodium glutamate. *Serves 5.*

BROCADE-LIKE ARRAY OF SEA FOOD, CHICKEN, AND VEGETABLES WITH NOODLES

Shih Chin T'ang Mien

5 cups chicken stock (see page 41)
1 teaspoon sesame oil
4 tablespoons soy
1½ teaspoons salt or more to suit taste
¼ cup green onion, julienned
2 tablespoons ginger root, julienned
½ cup chicken meat, julienned
½ cup prawns, deveined, washed, and cut in ½" pieces
¼ cup dried mushrooms (see page 36), julienned
¼ cup dried shrimp (see page 38)
3 pieces sea cucumbers (see page 37)
5 bowls boiled noodles

Heat the chicken stock over high heat and add other ingredients in order named, except noodles. Bring to a boil. Lower heat to medium and cook uncovered for 5 minutes. Pour the stock with the ingredients into bowls of noodles. *Serves 5.*

FRIED NOODLES

Ch'ao Mien

FRIED NOODLES WITH PRAWNS

Hsia Jen Ch'ao Mien

4 tablespoons sesame oil
½ cup green onion, chopped
2 tablespoons ginger root, chopped
1 pound prawns, deveined and washed
½ cup bamboo shoots (*see page 33*), julienned
4 tablespoons soy
½ teaspoon salt
1½ cups chicken stock (*see page 41*)
5 bowls boiled noodles

Bring the sesame oil to a boil over high heat, add onion, ginger, prawns, and bamboo shoots, and stir well. Add soy and salt and bring to a boil. Pour in the chicken stock, add the noodles, mix well, and cover. Reduce heat to low and simmer until hardly any liquid remains. Divide into 5 portions. Serve hot. *Serves 5.*

FRIED NOODLES IN BROCADE-LIKE ARRAY OF SEA FOOD, CHICKEN, AND VEGETABLES

Shih Chin Ch'ao Mien

Use the same ingredients as for *Shih Chin T'ang Mien* except stock (page *212*) but fry the ingredients in 4 table-spoons of sesame oil for 3 minutes. Add noodles and 1½ cups chicken stock. Simmer over medium heat uncovered until hardly any liquid remains. Serve hot. *Serves 5.*

NOODLES WITH SAUCE

Pan Mien

SPECIAL SAUCE WITH NOODLES

Ta Lu Pan Mien

½ pound pork, lean and fat
2 tablespoons dried shrimp (see page 38)
¼ cup green onion, chopped
2 tablespoons ginger root, chopped
½ cup dried mushrooms (see page 36), julienned
½ cup bamboo shoots (see page 33)
4 tablespoons soy
1 teaspoon salt or more to suit taste
5 cups pork stock (see page 42)
3 tablespoons cornstarch dissolved in ½ cup water
3 eggs, beaten
5 bowls boiled noodles

Place pork in a pot, add enough water to submerge the pork, and bring to a boil over high heat. Lower the heat to medium and simmer covered until well done. Remove pork and julienne into 1″ × 1/8″ × 1/8″ strips. Place in pot pork, shrimp, onion, ginger, mushrooms, bamboo shoots, soy, salt, and pork stock and bring to a boil over high heat. Lower the heat to medium and cook for 10 minutes covered. Add cornstarch paste and simmer until thickened. Add eggs and cook 1 minute. Pour the sauce over noodles. Serve hot. *Serves 5.*

FRIED SOY BEAN PASTE SAUCE WITH NOODLES

Cha Chiang Pan Mien

4 tablespoons sesame oil
½ pound pork, lean and fat in ½" cubes
2 tablespoons dried shrimp (see page 38)
¼ cup green onion, chopped
½ cup green onion, julienned 1" × ⅛"
1 tablespoon ginger root, chopped
1 cup sweet brown soy bean paste (see page 38)
1 tablespoon sugar
2 cups water
1 cup fresh soy beans, boiled
½ cup radish, julienned 1" × ⅛" × ⅛"
½ cup bean sprouts, both ends removed
½ cup cucumbers, julienned 1" × ⅛" × ⅛"
5 bowls noodles

Bring the sesame oil to boil in a pan over high heat and add pork, shrimp, chopped onion, and ginger. Fry for a few minutes, add soy bean paste, sugar, and water. Mix well, bring to a boil over high heat, then lower heat to medium and simmer, stirring constantly, until the paste is smooth. Place in a bowl. Put in 5 separate dishes each of the following ingredients: soy beans, bean sprouts, cucumbers, julienned onions, and radish, and place on the table surrounding the bean paste sauce. Serve the 5 bowls boiled noodles. Guests top the noodles with a large spoonful or more of bean paste sauce and a little of each of the five vegetables. Mix thoroughly before eating. *Serves 5.*

STEAMED BREADS

Cheng Shih

Cheng shih is a steamed raised dough made into many kinds of buns, with or without filling. A flour product and a staple in the North, it was considered a snack in the court and was made by the dessert section. On the following pages four kinds are described: buns without filling, rolls, buns with filling, and triangular steamed buns with filling. The basic dough recipe appears first.

RAISED DOUGH

Fa Mien

1 ⅓ *tablespoons dried yeast*
5 *cups sifted flour*
2 *cups water*

Dissolve yeast in ¼ cup warm water and add to the flour. Mix well and add 1¾ cups water and knead well for 7 to 8 minutes into a smooth dough. Let stand in a bowl for about 2 hours in a warm place until the bulk is doubled. Fold the sides toward the center and repeat the process until all the air is out.

BUNS WITHOUT FILLING

Man T'ou

Shape the dough into a roll of 24″ long, 2″ diameter, and cut into 2″ pieces. Shape the pieces into round flat-bottomed buns. Let stand to rise again to not quite double. Bring the water in the steamer to a boil and when the steamer has become piping hot, place a piece of dampened cloth on the bottom of the steaming basket and the buns on the cloth, leaving enough space for the buns to expand. Cover and steam for 15 minutes. Serve hot. *Serves 12.*

ROLLS

Hua Chüan

Roll and press the raised dough into two sheets ⅛″ thick. Sprinlcle each sheet with ½ teaspoon of salt, and brush entire surface with 1 tablespoon of sesame or other vegetable oil. Roll like a scroll into a bar of 18″ long and 1½″ diameter. Cut into 3″ bars and press the center with thick chopsticks to open out the cut ends. Let stand to rise again to not quite double. Bring the water in the steamer to boil over high heat and steam as above for 15 minutes. *Serves 12.*

BUNS WITH FILLING

Pao Tzu

Form raised dough into 2 rolls each 20″ long and 1″ diameter, and cut into 1″ pieces. Roll and press into 4½″ diameter round flat pieces. Place 1½ heaping teaspoons filling in the center and wrap into flat bottomed balls as shown in the illustration below. Steam as above for 20 minutes. Serve hot. Use fillings described on pages 195-98. *Serves 20.*

TRIANGULAR STEAMED BUNS WITH FILLING

San Chiao

Use half recipe for raised dough. Form a roll of 20″ long and 1″ diameter and cut into ½″ pieces. Roll and press the dough into flat round cakes 1/8″ thick and 1½″ to 2″ diameter. Place 1 heaping teaspoon red bean or date filling in the center of the cake and seal in a triangular shape as illustrated below. Steam in a steamer as in preceding recipe for 15 minutes. Serve hot. *Serves 20.*

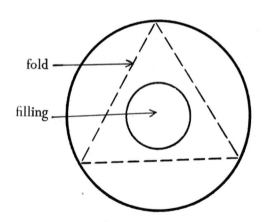

fold

filling

RED BEAN FILLING

Teng Sha Hsien

1 cup small red beans, picked and washed
3 cups water
½ tablespoon lard (other shortening may be substituted)
4 tablespoons sugar

Place beans in a pot with water and boil for 1 hour covered over medium heat until tender. Purée the beans. Melt the lard in a pan over medium heat, remove pan from the fire, and put in the puréed beans. Mix well and add sugar. Mix well, return the pan to fire, and stir continuously until the sugar has dissolved into the puréed bean. Add more water to the beans if necessary.

PURÉED DATES

Tsao Ni Hsien

1 pound Chinese dates, dried and washed
3 cups water
½ tablespoon lard (other shortening may be substituted)
4 tablespoons sugar

Boil dates in a pot with 3 cups water uncovered over medium heat for 1 hour or until hardly any water remains. Purée the dates. Melt lard in a pan, remove from fire and add the purée of dates and 4 tablespoons sugar. Mix well, return to fire, and stir continuously until the sugar has dissolved into the puréed dates.

MISCELLANEOUS SNACKS

Tza

On July 5, 1619, when the Manchurian army led by the first emperor of the Ch'ing Dynasty, encamped on the Manchurian bank of the River Ch'ing near the Great Wall, farmers in the neighborhood offered doves, Chinese cabbage, leaves of beefsteak plant, and rice to the emperor. Greatly pleased with the offerings, he ordered them to be cooked, and he enjoyed boiled rice mixed with dove meat, wrapped in leaves. In memory of this event and the hardships suffered during the formative years of his dynasty, the emperor ordered the Manchurian princes to eat this food every year on the 5th of July. Thus was founded a Manchurian custom which has been observed ever since. Originally this dish was prepared simply, but was gradually enhanced. Empress Dowager Tzu-hsi developed it into a very fancy dish for she minced and seasoned the dove meat instead of merely using it in plain roasted form. It was at this time that it was renamed *Ts'ai Pao Ke Sung* instead of *Ts'ai Pao*.

VEGETABLE ROLLS WITH MINCED DOVE

Ts'ai Pao Ke Sung

5 tablespoons sesame oil
½ teaspoon salt or more to suit taste
5 eggs, beaten
½ pound roasted dove meat, chopped (substitute quail)
½ pound Chinese ham, julienned
2 cups rice, boiled—avoid sticky, soft rice—(see page 37)
15 Chinese cabbage or lettuce leaves, washed and drained
15 beefsteak plant leaves (see page 34), washed and drained
4 tablespoons sesame paste (see page 38)

Bring the sesame oil to a boil over high heat in a pan, add salt to beaten eggs, and fry both sides until brown. Remove from the pan and break to pieces with chopsticks. Mix well the dove meat, Chinese ham, and eggs with cooked rice, without kneading, and put in a deep dish. On each cabbage leaf put a beefsteak leaf, spread with sesame paste, and place the hot rice mixture on top. Fold neatly into a roll and serve. *Serves 5–6.*

FESTIVAL DUMPLINGS

Yuan Hsiao

Yuan Hsiao is a kind of snack or dessert, eaten on the evening of the *Yuan Hsiao* Festival, on the 15th of January, the first festival of the year. Since in China roundness is symbolic of fulfillment, peace, and domestic happiness, little round dumplings were made for everyone to start the new year in an optimistic spirit.

1 cup small red beans, picked and washed
6 cups water plus 3 cups
1 tablespoon lard (other shortening may be substituted)
7 tablespoons sugar or more to suit taste
3 cups glutinous rice powder

Place beans in a pot with 6 cups water and boil for 1 hour and 15 minutes over medium heat covered. Purée the beans. Melt the lard in a pan over medium heat, remove pan from fire and put in purée beans. Mix well, add sugar and again mix well. Return pan to fire and stir continuously until the sugar has dissolved into the bean paste. Form the paste into a 6″ square and cool until hardened. Dust cutting board with flour, place the bean paste square on the board, and cut into ½″ cubes. Dip 4 to 5 cubes in water and place them in a large bowl of glutinous rice flour. Swirl the cubes until they are coated with a layer of flour. Dip them in water and repeat the process until the balls become 1″ in diameter. Bring medium-sized pot half filled with water to a boil over high heat and put in rice floured balls. Cook until the water comes to a boil then add 1 cup water and repeat the process 3 times. Remove balls from the pot and serve. In the imperial court 5 balls were served in a bowl to each guest. Serve hot. Puréed Dates (see page 221) and Haws Jelly (see page 148, Steamed Lotus Seed recipe) are both delectable and may be substituted for red bean paste.

FLOUR FRIED WITH BUTTER

Niu Yu Ch'ao Mien

One would think that it is only recently that instant foods have been invented, but the following recipe was originated 600 years ago by the Mongols. It was used by Genghis Khan and his men as a field ration, and they carried it in their pouches during their numerous invasions.

2 tablespoons butter
1 ¼ cups flour
4 tablespoons sugar
2 ½ tablespoons sesame
¼ cup walnut meats, chopped
1 ½ tablespoons watermelon seeds, shelled

Melt butter in a pan over medium heat and add other ingredients. Fry, stirring constantly, until the flour turns a light brown. Put 4 tablespoons of mixture in a bowl and mix with 2½ to 3 tablespoons water to form the paste which the Mongols used to eat as field ration. A drop of vanilla added to the paste makes a delicious filling for meringue shells and can be used for dessert. Four tablespoons of prepared flour paste fills 5 meringue shells of 1″ diameter. The prepared flour may be bottled and refrigerated for future use.

COOKED DRIED FRUITS

Kuo Tzu Kan

Both in the court and among the citizenry, the following dish was a summer favorite.

1¾ *cups dried persimmons, washed, cut* 1″ × ½″ × ⅛″
4 *cups water*
10 *dried Chinese dates, washed*
¾ *cup lotus root, fresh and tender, washed, cut* 1″ × ½″ × ⅛″
3 *tablespoons sugar*
1 *tablespoon rose essence (see page 37)*

Bring to a boil 2 cups water in a pot and simmer persimmons uncovered over low heat for 20 minutes. In another pot bring to a boil 2 cups water and simmer dates uncovered over low heat for 30 minutes. Add dates and lotus roots to persimmons. Add sugar and rose essence and stir gently. Simmer over low heat uncovered for another 10 minutes. Serve hot or cold. *Serves 5–6.*

ALMOND TEA

Hsing Jen Cha

Hsing Jen Cha was enjoyed in the court and was also very popular among the people. It is said to be very good for sore throats.

1 cup rice, washed
½ pound almonds, blanched
6 cups water
5 tablespoons sugar

Place the rice and almonds in a pot, add water and soak for 8 hours. Drain. Grind the rice and almonds in a grinder. Add enough water gradually to maintain a liquidy paste-like consistency. Boil the rice and almond liquid in a pot, stirring constantly, for 30 minutes. A double boiler is recommended to prevent scorching. Add sugar. Mix well, and bring to a boil. Serve hot. *Serves 8–10.*

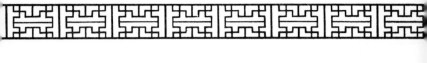

PICKLES

PICKLES

Hsien Ts'ai

Pickles are eaten with meals or sweets to sharpen the palate. They consist mostly of vegetables and are briny, sour, sweet, or spicy. Soochow, Yangchow, Hunan, and Peking were known for their delicious pickles. In the court, pickles were made in a special kitchen under the superintendence of the vegetable section of the imperial kitchen, and there were over 250 kinds. They were made in so great a quantity that those recipes which can be adapted in an ordinary home are limited. However, I am including three varieties.

FIVE SPICES DRIED SUGAR BEETS

Wu Hsiang Lo Pa Kan

1 pound sugar beets, washed and quartered (carrots or radishes may be substituted)
¼ cup salt
1 teaspoon Five Spices
1 teaspoon sesame oil or more to suit taste
1 teaspoon vinegar or more to suit taste

Dry quarters of sugar beets in the sun until half-dried. Rub salt into the beets and place them out in the sun to dry thoroughly. Mold will form if not thoroughly dried. Rub Five Spices into the beets when they are completely dried. Place them in a jar, cover, and seal. Let stand for a month. Take out the desired amount of pickles from the jar, wash, and steep in hot water for 20 minutes until tender. Cut in 1″ × 1/8″ × 1/8″ pieces. Place in a dish and add a mixture of sesame oil and vinegar. *Serves 10–12.*

SUGAR BEETS CURED IN RED PEPPER PASTE

Chiang Lo Pa

1 pound sugar beets, washed, quartered (radishes may be substituted)
1 quart red pepper paste (see page 37)
2 cups sugar

Dehydrate the sugar beet quarters in the sun. Partially fill a medium sized jar with pepper paste, add sugar, and mix well. Place the beet quarters in the paste and submerge well. Cover and seal and let stand for 2 months. Take out desired amount of beets, wash, and cut in ½″ cubes. *Serves 12–14.*

VEGETABLES PICKLED IN BRINE

Pao Ts'ai

6 cups water

1½ cups salt

2 pounds Chinese cabbage, washed, drained, dried with a cloth, and quartered

½ pound carrots, washed, drained, dried with a cloth, and halved

½ pound string beans, washed, drained, cleaned, and dried with a cloth

5 pieces red cayenne pepper, dried

1 teaspoon sesame oil or more to suit taste

Prepare a brine of 6 cups water and 1½ cups salt and bring to a boil over high heat. After it has cooled, pour into a sterilized jar. Add the cabbage, carrots, string beans, and cayenne peppers. Cover and let stand 1 week. Take out the desired amount of pickles with sterilized chopsticks or a fork. Chop fine without washing. Serve in a dish with sesame oil. More vegetables may be added after they have been washed and dried with a cloth. *Serves 30 or more.*

PROVISIONERS

Bombay Emporium, Ltd.
12 Martello Street
London, E. 8

Ti Hang Lung & Co.
846 Grant Avenue
San Francisco 8, California

Oriental Food Shop
1302 Amsterdam Avenue
New York 27, N.Y.

Berkeley Campus Coop
University of Calif.
Berkeley, California

Mee Wah Lung Co.
608 H. Street N.W.
Washington, D.C.

Kwong Wah Chong Co.
938 Maunakea Street
Honolulu, Hawaii

Red and Blue Co.
2247 Wentworth Avenue
Chicago 16, Illinois

Yuen Chong Co., Ltd.
83 North King Street
Honolulu, Hawaii

Yee Sing Chong Co.
960–962 North Hill Street
Los Angeles 12, California

Kasho Boeki Yugen Kaisha
185 Yamashita-cho
Yokohama, Japan

Sam Ward Co., Inc.
957–961 North Hill Street
Los Angeles 12, California

Chunichi Shokuin Co., Ltd.
No. 2 Kamiya-cho
Shiba, Minato-ku
Tokyo, Japan

Superior Trading Company
867 Washington Street
San Francisco 8, California

INDEX